Contents

Cover: Columbia (symbol of the
United States) depicted armless and
impotent as the flames of the
First World War approach
Front endpaper: Wartime British
postcard looks forward to the coming
of America's armies
Rear endpaper: Wilson with King
George V on a visit to England, 1918

Copyright © 1972: Edmund Ions
First published in 1972 by Macdonald
St Giles House 49 Poland St London W1
in the British Commonwealth and
American Heritage Press
551 Fifth Avenue New York NY 10017
in the United States of America
Library of Congress Card Catalogue
Number: 77-37602
Made and printed in Great Britain by
Purnell & Sons Ltd Paulton Somerset

WOODROW WILSON

The Politics of Peace and War

Edmund Ions

Library of the 20th Century
Macdonald/American Heritage

Prologue
Triumph and Tragedy

Woodrow Wilson's life falls into three well-defined stages: the scholar, the politician, and the statesman. His political career was one of early triumph and final tragedy. This book concentrates on his political career, his war-time diplomacy, and the final destruction of his hopes after the First World War.

It is a story rich in lessons for the student of history and politics. He brought to his political career immense gifts: scholarly perception and a passion for seeking the truth, high ideals and a genuine wish to improve the condition of the people, the conscience of a devout Christian whose settled habit it was to read a chapter from the Bible each evening before retiring to bed, some of the astuteness, even the canniness, of the Scotch-Presbyterian stock from which he was drawn, and political courage of the first order.

As a politician, however, he had defects and shortcomings, some of them the product of his more virtuous qualities: a certain inflexibility, a strain of stubbornness, and a tendency to regard the political arguments of his opponents as personal attacks upon himself. He was easily wounded, and some of his critics would suggest that he lacked the power of decision. In the American Presidency, such a defect is a serious one, for events do not wait upon Presidents, least of all in time of war.

Woodrow Wilson took office at a momentous period in the fortunes of the American Republic. The spirit of Progressivism, with its spate of reforming zeal, was still abroad in the land. The trail blazed by President Theodore Roosevelt had by no means eradicated the social and political evils created in the second half of the 19th century. The tide of immigration from Europe — those 'huddled masses, yearning to breathe free' — had deposited millions of poverty-stricken Europeans on America's doorstep in successive decades. As the cities mushroomed, so their problems multiplied. The ready availability of cheap labour led to exploitation, corruption, and jobbery in municipal politics. When industrial capital was combined

Left: *Woodrow Wilson (1856-1924), apostle of US democracy*

5

with the vast resources of America for the first time, huge fortunes were made by those who used their wealth to consolidate their hold on the economic and then on the political system of the United States.

Problems enough at home then to test the abilities of any President. And Wilson's task was made enormously greater by America's growing entanglement in the mighty conflict which broke out in Europe in 1914 — an entanglement which led inexorably to the United States becoming one of the belligerents. When the First World War was over and Germany defeated, Wilson went to Paris to help make peace. It was a time of bitterness and disillusionment for him as he witnessed what seemed to him just that spirit of greed and narrow nationalism which had provoked the war. At one moment he threatened to leave, but he stayed, and managed to rescue from the vengeful settlement of Versailles the Covenant of the League of Nations, a cause for which he now gave all his energies and eventually his health.

The American Senate later voted against American membership of the League of Nations. The cause on which he had set his heart was lost. Commentators at the time remarked that without American membership the League would be incapable of preserving the peace, least of all the fragile peace bought in Europe by means of a punitive settlement on a defeated Germany. A decade later this pessimism proved to be well founded. Within twenty years Europe had embarked on the Second World War.

His failure and disappointment at the end may suggest that he left no monument. But as the Second World War came to an end and the representatives of forty-six nations met at San Francisco to draft the Charter of a United Nations Organisation, they were in effect paying homage to the spirit of the statesman who had striven so hard to bequeath a very similar organisation to a shattered Europe and a disorganised world in 1919. On the centenary of Woodrow Wilson's birth in 1956 a tribute was paid by the Secretary-General of the United Nations as he unveiled a bust and tablet in commemoration of the dead statesman. The speech recalled that Woodrow Wilson had urged the creation of an organisation which should be 'not merely a formal thing, not an occasional thing', but one with a 'vital continuity . . . the eye of the nations to keep watch upon the common interest'. If we look for a monument to Woodrow Wilson's ideals and his vision, we can find it in the United Nations Organisation, which has played a vital part in keeping peace between the great powers for a quarter of a century.

Left: Paradoxically, in the Presidency of a man of peace, the United States enthusiastically entered the First World War

7

Chapter 1
The Preacher's Son

Thomas Woodrow Wilson was born in a manse in Virginia, though his birth was more humble and his upbringing more austere than this fact suggests. His father, Joseph Ruggles Wilson, was a Presbyterian preacher who had moved from Ohio to Staunton in Virginia in 1855. His mother, Jessie Woodrow, was born in England, herself the daughter of a Presbyterian minister.

When Joseph Wilson became minister of the First Presbyterian Church in Staunton he took up residence in the manse, part of his benefice, and it was here that his son, the future President of the United States, was born on 28th December 1856. The family moved to Augusta, Georgia about a year later. Woodrow Wilson later recalled that his first memory, when he was nearly four years old, was of hearing someone passing his father's house saying anxiously that Mr Lincoln had been elected and there was to be a war.

When the Civil War came, the Reverend Joseph Wilson supported the Southern cause against the Northern Yankees. Scenes in both the church and the family home must have resembled those from *Gone With The Wind*, as the church was transformed into a hospital and the churchyard into a stockade for Yankee prisoners. The sight of bloodshed and suffering undoubtedly marked young Woodrow.

Woodrow Wilson was a studious boy. Naturally he was familiar with the Bible, both at home and in his father's church. Dickens and Sir Walter Scott also figured among the family readings at home, helping to shape the mind and literary abilities of the schoolboy. At the age of seventeen, Woodrow went off to a small Presbyterian college in North Carolina. He shone in the debating club, even though he was a shy and reserved student, and he wrote a new constitution for the club.

In September 1875 he went on to Princeton, a private college in the New Jersey countryside, which was not particularly distinguished for learning but preserved an atmosphere of Southern gentility, despite its proximity

Left: The twenty-eighth President as a Princeton undergraduate

9

to the urban East Coast. And Wilson continued to defend the Southern cause in the Civil War and found most of his friends among men from the South. The peacefulness of Princeton village appealed deeply to him, although his first year at the college was not distinguished, and he found the work taxing. His second year saw a sudden rapid development: one of his biographers called it among the most formative and important in his life. It was certainly a turning point, and from then on the scholar's life seemed to beckon.

Wilson was reading avidly in politics and history. He formed a lasting admiration for the works of the British historian Macaulay and the political philosophers Edmund Burke and Walter Bagehot. Classics such as *The Federalist,* in which his own countrymen had debated the principles of the American Republic after the Revolution, equally fascinated him. At the same time he was taking a full part in debating, and even formed a society of his own during his years at Princeton. He published an article on Bismarck during his second year as a student, and followed this with a prize essay on another European statesman, the elder Pitt. His interest in politics was both academic and practical, and to his close friends and contemporaries he confided his intention of entering political life. Once or twice he amused himself by writing out cards headed 'Thomas Woodrow Wilson, Senator from Virginia'. At other times he settled for the Governorship of the State in his private scribblings.

Wilson's loyalties to the South may seem somewhat surprising in view of his later career. But his devotion to his father, his affection for the old-fashioned courtesies of the ordinary folk of Virginia, not to mention his dislike of the money-grubbing and materialistic qualities of the 'damn Yankees', help to explain it. On graduating from Princeton he returned to Virginia, and enrolled at the University of Virginia to study law. Once more he took a full part in student debating and orated on various topical issues, from nationalism and Free Trade to the power of the Roman Catholic Church, arguing on the latter subject that Roman Catholicism was not a menace to American civilisation.

He enjoyed debating more than he did his law course. In a letter to a friend in 1879 he confessed that he was 'most terribly bored by the noble study of the Law'. However, he still kept up his reading in his favourite subjects: history, political science, and literature. Indeed, he worked so hard that his health suffered and ultimately he was forced to return home, where he pursued his

Right: 1883 — Marietta Street, Atlanta, Georgia, where Wilson had his law office. The crowd has gathered to watch the funeral of A.H.Stephens, Vice-President of the Southern Confederacy

studies in the more relaxed surroundings of his parents' new home at Wilmington. It was during this period that he decided to go into practice, and in 1882, after discussing it with his father, he tried to set up a partnership in Atlanta with a friend from the University of Virginia. But the fledgling firm did not prosper.

Love and learning

The young lawyer was now twenty-six and unmarried, but in 1883, on a visit to Rome, Georgia, he met Ellen Louise Axson, an art student and the daughter of a Presbyterian minister. The courtship was rapid — in fact whirlwind for those days. In less than six months the couple were engaged and Wilson found new depths of experience in the love and devotion shared by the happy couple. Meanwhile, the problem of his professional future still remained, and since the practice of law was proving unrewarding in every sense of the word, Woodrow Wilson enrolled in the graduate school of the Johns Hopkins University at Baltimore.

It was a happy choice. The university was in a period of intense intellectual activity, and the graduate seminars under Herbert Baxter Adams, T. Franklin Jameson, and other great teachers were already becoming famous well beyond Baltimore. Initially Wilson did not enjoy the seminars, nor even the teaching and content of the courses conducted by Adams. But eventually he settled down, threw himself into his studies, and concentrated on the study of American government. He still admired the writings of Walter Bagehot, in particular the Englishman's great work *The English Constitution* (1867) which had established itself as a classic on both sides of the Atlantic. But Woodrow Wilson's ability and aptitude had now reached a stage where he could himself make an original contribution to the study of government. In 1884 he completed the manuscript of a book on American government which was to earn him a marked reputation as a scholar. The book was quickly published by a Boston firm, and almost as soon as it appeared, under the title *Congressional Government,* it was hailed as a minor classic. In it he examined the balance of forces and institutions operating in the American Constitution. He showed acute insight into the strengths and weaknesses of the United States Senate and the House of Representatives, as well as analysing the relationships between the Presidency and the legislature. During the last half century the reputation of the book has declined, and some scholars have noted shortcomings. But at the time its reception was extremely favourable.

Left: Faculty and students at Bryn Mawr College. Professor Woodrow Wilson is standing on the extreme right of the top row

The result was that Woodrow Wilson was looked upon as a potential scholar. With mixed feelings his steps turned towards academic life. Professors could not really participate in active politics, he had already acknowledged to a friend, so he must content himself with being merely 'an *outside* force in politics'. Beyond that, he hoped that eventually he might aspire to 'an active, if possible a leading part in public life, and . . . if I had the ability, a *statesman's* career'. The young scholar was not without ambition, therefore, and the life of politics still beckoned.

In June 1885 he married Ellen Axson, and that September they went to Bryn Mawr, a ladies' college in Pennsylvania, where Woodrow Wilson had been appointed to teach history and government. Married life brought deep and lasting contentment, but he did not enjoy his spell at Bryn Mawr. During his third year of teaching at the austere little college among the woods of Pennsylvania he wrote to a friend that he was 'hungry for a class of *men*'. When an offer came from a men's university, Wesleyan University in Connecticut, Wilson accepted with alacrity and took Ellen there in the summer of 1888. He had still not lost his old love of debating, and among other activities he helped the students to found a 'Wesleyan House of Commons'. He was also still writing a good deal and published *The State* during his time at Wesleyan. The book provides interesting clues to Wilson's emergent political philosophy. He agreed with Edmund Burke that revolutions are always followed by severe regimes, often enough by an even greater tyranny. With Walter Bagehot and Herbert Spencer he held that man's political evolution and the growth of human institutions was 'scarcely less coherent and orderly than those of the physical world'. Government must be, in the last analysis, based on 'organised force'. In every society there must be governors and the governed. The young professor was to rediscover the truth of these nostrums only too clearly, sometimes painfully, in the decades which lay ahead.

In the meantime, ambition had not departed with his translation to Wesleyan. In 1890 he received a call from his *alma mater* and accepted the chair of jurisprudence and political economy at Princeton. He was now a notable figure in the academic life of East Coast America. Several universities offered him presidencies, including three invitations from the University of Virginia. He declined each and all, but when Princeton offered him her presidency in 1902 he accepted. Academically he had now

Left: Cartoon mocks Democrat William Jennings Bryan's 'cross of gold' speech—Wilson supported Bryan's candidature in the Presidential election of 1896, but without much enthusiasm

Woodrow Wilson's America

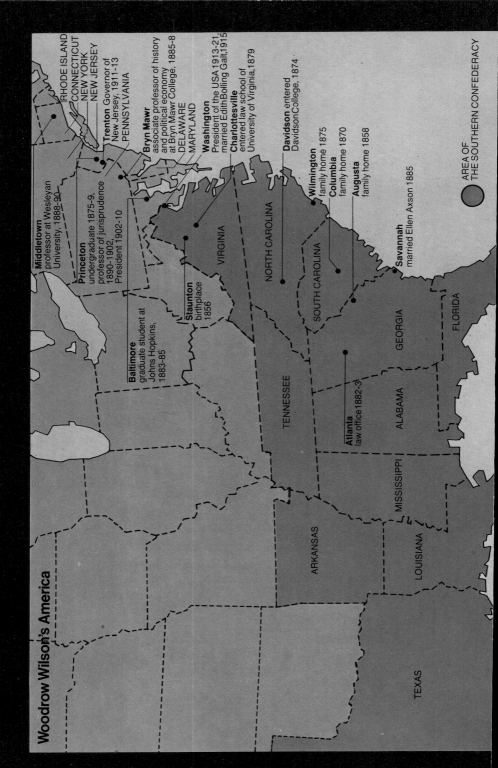

RHODE ISLAND
CONNECTICUT
NEW YORK
NEW JERSEY

Trenton Governor of New Jersey, 1911-13
PENNSYLVANIA

Bryn Mawr associate professor of history and political economy at Bryn Mawr College, 1885-8
DELAWARE
MARYLAND

Washington President of the USA 1913-21, married EdithBolling Galt,1915

Charlottesville entered law school of University of Virginia,1879

Davidson entered DavidsonCollege, 1874

Wilmington family home 1875

Columbia family home 1870

Augusta family home 1858

Savannah married Ellen Axson 1885

Middletown professor at Wesleyan University, 1888-90

Princeton undergraduate 1875-9, professor of jurisprudence 1890-1902, President 1902-10

Baltimore graduate student at Johns Hopkins, 1883-85

Staunton birthplace 1856

Atlanta law office 1882-3

VIRGINIA

NORTH CAROLINA

SOUTH CAROLINA

GEORGIA

FLORIDA

TENNESSEE

ALABAMA

ARKANSAS

MISSISSIPPI

LOUISIANA

TEXAS

AREA OF THE SOUTHERN CONFEDERACY

definitely arrived, in every sense of the word.

His interest in politics and the possibilities of a political career had never entirely deserted him. Politically the 1890s had been one of the liveliest decades in American history. The nation had once more been riven by sectionalism, this time in the gold and silver controversy. In the Mid-West and West, the farmers had revolted against the financial power of the East. At the heart of the matter was the demand of the 'silverites' of the Western states that free coinage of silver should be maintained in the American monetary system. The supporters of a single currency, tied to gold, flourished in Wall Street and the financial capitals of East Coast America. The silver cause found a fiery spokesman in William Jennings Bryan. When the Democratic Party assembled in uneasy convention in 1896 at Chicago — in the heartland of America — Bryan brought the delegates to their feet with his crusading challenge to the gold speculators of the East Coast: 'You shall not press down upon the brow of labour this crown of thorns, you shall not crucify mankind upon a cross of gold.'

The speech had a rapturous reception among delegates from the agrarian West and South, and Bryan won the Presidential nomination for the coming elections. But the Democratic Party was split and in November the Republican, William McKinley, won the Presidency. With a Republican installed in the White House for a term of four years, the Democratic Party could only lick its wounds and worry about its future as a national party. In 1900 McKinley again defeated the Democrats. His Vice-President was the ambitious and energetic Theodore Roosevelt. A year later McKinley was assassinated and Roosevelt became President. The era of Progressive reform had begun.

As a Democrat, Woodrow Wilson watched with mixed feelings as the events of a troubled decade unfolded. He voted for the Democratic ticket in 1896, but he was no admirer of William Jennings Bryan. He thought the 'cross of gold' speech at Chicago ridiculous, and deplored the strident demagogy which he felt he saw in the man. To Bryan, of course, Woodrow Wilson (if indeed he had heard of him) was merely an 'ivory tower' academic, cloistered in the quiet little township of Princeton, New Jersey. Neither man could remotely have guessed that in twelve years' time Bryan would be appointed Secretary of State by President Thomas Woodrow Wilson.

Left: Woodrow Wilson's background was essentially provincial and small town. Yet the nation which elected him its President was becoming increasingly dominated by its vast urban centres

Chapter 2
Princeton's President

Princeton invited many notable figures to witness Wilson's inauguration on 25th October 1902. Among the guests were Grover Cleveland, twice President of the United States in the 1890s, literary figures such as Mark Twain and William Dean Howells, the banker J. Pierpont Morgan, and the Negro leader Booker T. Washington. The quiet lawns of Princeton had rarely seen such an array of eminent figures from the world of politics, literature, and public affairs.

Woodrow Wilson had ambitious plans to bring Princeton into the front rank of the nation's educational establishments. He set his sights high. 'In planning for Princeton . . . we are planning for the country,' he declared at his installation. His prime aim was to raise the intellectual calibre of the university, and he introduced what was termed the 'preceptorial' system to the teaching. This corresponded closely to the tutorial system at Oxford and Cambridge in England, where rather than maintaining formal or distant relationships between the teacher and the taught, the tutors gave guidance and personal friendship as well as supervision. Wilson also reorganised the faculty into four divisions, with a good deal of flexibility within each division in order to break down the rigid compartments which marked the old system. These reforms took time. The new president suffered some defeats against the entrenched interests of some of the professors. Wilson's recruitment of able professors from elsewhere was also received with mixed feelings. But after three years of intense work and not a few internal battles, the new president's reforms were taking root, and Princeton's name and reputation began to spread well beyond the State of New Jersey. Wilson received, and deserved, chief credit.

But the course of the president's reforming zeal did not run altogether smoothly and he lost a major battle which not only throws much light on his ideals and beliefs, but shows the streak of stubbornness that was to prove a

Left: Student cartoon claims that Wilson's pursuit of academic excellence will decimate Princeton's easy-going student body

major tragedy at the end of his career. The battle involved the eating clubs at Princeton. Students were elected to these after their freshman year, when their acceptability had been vetted or appraised by senior students. Some clubs were highly exclusive, their membership restricted to the wealthier or socially well-connected students. Poorer students were often not elected to any eating club, and had to find their meals as best they could in a nearby town. Their situation, in the words of Woodrow Wilson, was 'little less than deplorable'. He proposed to replace the eating clubs by a 'Quadrangle' plan, where students would be housed, fed, and would take their recreation and campus social life in common rooms, again on the model of the Oxford and Cambridge colleges.

Defeat for Wilson

The plan met with bitter opposition from Princeton alumni, who were powerfully represented on the Board of Trustees. If the new Quad plan was to be installed, the first need was for considerable sums of money for new buildings. This again depended on donations from the alumni. Wilson made strenuous appeals, but now he met bitter opposition from his own faculty, many of them with sentimental ties to the Princeton they had known for many years. Wilson could possibly have won his battle if he had been prepared to compromise, perhaps allowing the eating clubs to continue alongside a modified Quad plan. But he refused. To Wilson the eating clubs represented privilege and exclusiveness. He wanted to be rid of them. The alumni and the Board of Trustees stood firm and he lost the battle.

In the course of the bitter personal feuding which went on over this issue, Woodrow Wilson was engaged in another battle concerning the location of the new graduate college on the campus. In this, as in the Quad plan dispute, his stubbornness and inability to compromise inflamed the controversy. The president won this particular battle, but in doing so he alienated many friends on the faculty by his intransigence, not to mention his tendency to cast issues of principle in terms of declarations of loyalty to himself as president.

These quarrels seriously impaired Wilson's relations with many of his colleagues, including senior professors and powerful trustees like Grover Cleveland. Wilson's health had also been impaired by the continued strain and overwork. After eight years at Princeton he was ready for a change. But where could he go? In academic life he could hardly go up, unless it might be to the presidency of Harvard or Yale, or some other prestigious university. But Wilson had had his fill of academic politics and their internal feuding. His gaze wandered

PENNSYI

PRESIDENT W

FOOT

COLUMBIA

Prince

Octobe

SPECIA

Will leave TRENT

riving at PRINC

RETURNING, Leave

J. B. HUTCHINSON,   J. R. WOO
General Manager.   Gen'l Pass.
14-20-1902. 100.   Allen, Lane & Scott,

Pennsylvania Railroad poste

outside the narrow confines of academic groves.

Among Wilson's friends and admirers was a successful
journalist named George M. Harvey, editor of the influential *Harper's Weekly* and a friend of the banker J.
Pierpont Morgan. Harvey was convinced that he recognised true statesmanship and future greatness in Woodrow Wilson. He did not hesitate to use his editorial
columns to air his own views, and on one occasion in
1906 he printed a full-page picture of Wilson on the cover
of *Harper's Weekly*. Wilson was flattered by Harvey's
attentions, but embarrassed when Harvey and his friends
flighted the suggestion that Woodrow Wilson would
make an ideal President of the United States.

Certainly the Democratic Party lacked a standard
bearer who could compare with the bustling Theodore
Roosevelt, now holding the Presidential stage. Roosevelt
had captured the public imagination with his assault on
the trusts and monopolies which were fixing prices and
operating against that spirit of competitive free enterprise enshrined in the American system. After his vic-
torious 'trust-busting' campaign, Roosevelt was now
busily extending American influence overseas by his Far
Eastern policies. He had already ensured that the American navy should be enlarged to a position of supremacy
in the Pacific theatre, and elsewhere on the world stage
he staked America's claim to be recognised as a leading
power. In 1905 he had intervened between Russia and
Japan to bring the Russo-Japanese War to an end, and
received a Nobel peace prize in consequence. Apart from
his vigorous, even aggressive statesmanship, he captured the imagination of the American people by his combination of personal vigour, courage, and uncompromising
patriotism. The Democratic Party, it seemed, had no one
to match him.

Not surprisingly, therefore, Woodrow Wilson played
down the efforts of George Harvey to cast him in the role
of a potential President. He feared that talk of his candidacy would become a national joke. But if Presidential
politics were out for the present, perhaps Woodrow
Wilson could be persuaded to run for public office at a
less exalted level? The Governorship of New Jersey was
coming up for election in the autumn of 1910. New Jersey
politics were largely dominated by corrupt machine politicians at the time, and the results of their depredations
could be seen in cities such as Trenton and Newark. A new
broom was needed. Harvey decided that Woodrow Wilson
was just the man, and he set to work.

*Left: Perils of the Ivy League—Wilson's inauguration to the
college presidency gets smaller billing than the Big Game*

Chapter 3
To the White House

In his role as kingmaker 'Colonel' Harvey (the military title was merely decorative) first approached the most important man in New Jersey politics, James Smith Junior. A former United States Senator, an Irish immigrant who had raised himself from poverty and ignorance by his own bootstraps, Smith was almost the prototype political boss and fixer: shrewd, calculating – and ruthless when he had to be. He hankered to return to the Senate, and quickly recognised that a man like Woodrow Wilson would confer just the respectability that the New Jersey Democrats so notably lacked. And if, in turn, Smith could act as kingmaker for a future Democratic President, all the better for New Jersey and James Smith's hold on the politics of the state.

There was a problem, however. Some of Smith's lieutenants, the city bosses he had helped into power, would hardly welcome an austere professor in the Governor's mansion. Woodrow Wilson's unbending Christian morality might well be directed against the corrupt fiefdoms the city bosses had long fashioned for themselves from the rich pickings of municipal contracts and city treasuries.

Yet even they could not deny that Woodrow Wilson was a highly-esteemed man, with an impeccable pedigree, whose reputation now extended far beyond the borders of New Jersey. And in state politics, as in national politics, the vital thing was to select a candidate who could win. Policies could be worked out later by battles within the party. If the Republicans carried the Governorship in November 1910 there would be no pickings for Democrats either way.

In January 1910, over lunch at Delmonico's restaurant in New York, Colonel Harvey broached Wilson's candidacy to James Smith. The New Jersey boss was lukewarm at first, or merely cautious. He wanted to talk with his own aides. A week later, however, Smith seemed more keen. The political bosses had weighed the situation carefully. Harvey now turned to Woodrow Wilson. The Princeton

Left: Rhetoric and sincerity – the professor turns politician

president was deeply immersed in the internal quarrel over the location of the graduate school, but he received his friend and confidant at his home. A remarkable conversation followed. Harvey broached the topic which had brought him to Princeton. Woodrow Wilson was reluctant, but pensive. He was familiar with the seamy reputation of many of the New Jersey Democrats with whom he would be involved if he took up Harvey's suggestion. But Harvey had laid his plans carefully. He played his trump card: 'If I can handle the matter so that the nomination for Governor can be tendered to you on a silver platter without you turning a hand to obtain it . . . what do you think would be your attitude?'

Wilson paced the carpet in his study, deep in thought. Then he replied, 'If the nomination for Governor should come to me in that way, I should regard it as my duty to give the matter very serious consideration.'

It was an ambiguous and astute reply. Wilson was covering his retreat if it should prove necessary or desirable. But Harvey was satisfied. It was still early spring, and there was plenty of time to promote Woodrow Wilson's candidacy before the November election. Smith and his lieutenants had already agreed to swing the Democratic Party organisation behind Wilson if he accepted their nomination.

Some bargaining still had to be done. Promises were required from the candidate that he would make no attempt to dismantle the existing Democratic organisations in the cities and counties if he were elected Governor. Harvey acted as middle man in the negotiations, and with Wilson's promises conveyed, Smith warmed to the idea of his candidacy. By now Smith was positively seeing himself in the role of kingmaker at the Democratic convention in 1912, when the party would have to choose a candidate for the Presidency. Smith intended that Woodrow Wilson would be the claimant, calculating that he himself would then become a national figure.

Woodrow Wilson made his final decision in July, after many comings and goings between Harvey, himself, and Smith. To his academic friends Wilson remarked that, after all his urgings to Princeton men to accept the call to public duty if it should come, he did not see how he himself could decline it.

In November Woodrow Wilson was elected Governor of New Jersey by a majority of almost 50,000 over his Republican rival. 1910 was a good year for Democrats elsewhere. Many felt that the nation was beginning to tire of Theodore Roosevelt's 'Big Stick' adventurism abroad, which dragged the United States into the quarrels of

Right: *A whistle-stop for Wilson on the 1912 campaign trail*

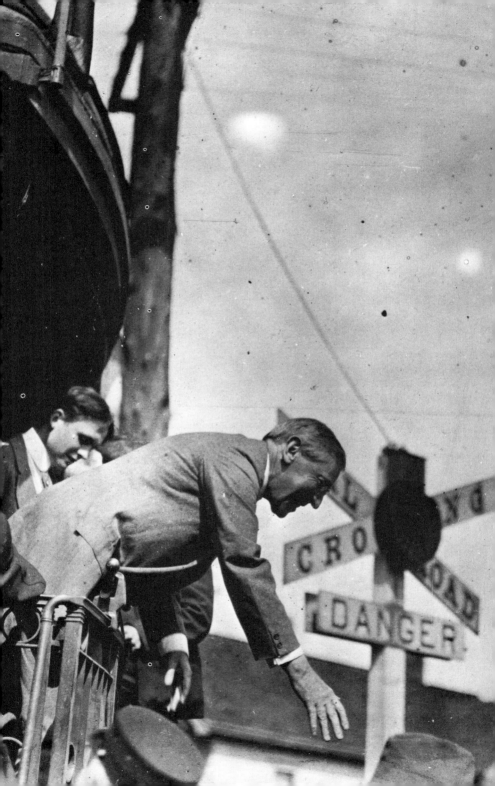

Europe. Already the war clouds were gathering over Europe, and efforts to stop the armaments race had proved fruitless. Indeed America herself was enlarging her navy and deeply involved in carving out spheres of influence in the Far East, whilst Germany and Britain jostled for African possessions. The rich, imperialist nations were dividing up the world, and the fact that the United States should be identified with the imperialist quest was an affront to many ordinary Americans who felt that this sort of adventurism might well drag America into a future confrontation between the colonialist powers of Europe.

In 1910 a Democratic majority was returned to the House of Representatives in the US Congress for the first time since 1892. In the normally Republican states of New York, Massachusetts, Connecticut, and Ohio, Democratic Governors were elected. In New Jersey, Woodrow Wilson had not merely wrested the Governorship from the Republicans, but he carried into the State Assembly a majority of Democrats to transform the balance of power in the state legislature. Wilson was now a national figure. Telegrams of congratulations from leading members of the Democratic Party arrived at Princeton, including one from William Jennings Bryan, the fiery Nebraskan who was to play a key role in Wilson's future career.

Woodrow Wilson also received strong support during the campaign from the liberal and progressive forces in New Jersey. These were largely made up of responsible citizens who were anxious to clean up the politics of the state, in particular to purge the corrupt city administrations who had milched city funds and used their connections at city halls to install their friends and accomplices in key positions. If the new Governor was not to alienate the progressive elements in the state — Republicans as well as Democrats — he had to move against the worst elements in the Democratic organisations. This was Woodrow Wilson's first major political test, and he did not shirk it.

The election over, Boss James Smith confidently expected his reward. He wished to return to the United States Senate. At this time members of the Senate were elected by state legislatures, a practice which ceased with an Amendment to the Constitution three years later, when popular election replaced this indirect method. With the Governor's endorsement in the state legislature, Smith could thus count on returning to the Senate. But Woodrow Wilson declined to give his endorsement. At the later stages of the 1910 campaign he had indicated that he intended to root out corruption in state politics, even though he was careful not to name names at that

stage. Now that he was installed in office, Wilson began to prove that he was as good as his word. Smith's was the first head to fall. The Governor put forward an alternative candidate for the Senate, and after a bitter and protracted battle in the legislature, Smith admitted defeat.

'Presidential timber'

This victory spurred Woodrow Wilson to other measures. He introduced and passed election laws which took power away from the city bosses by placing the selection of candidates in the hands of the ordinary voters by means of primary elections. A Corrupt Practices Act brought into the statute book more legislation aimed at ridding the state of corruption in both the political and business spheres. The Governor then showed his concern for working people by bringing forward an employers' liability act. Other measures too demonstrated the genuinely progressive and reforming temper of his administration. By the time the Democratic Party assembled for its national convention in 1912, Woodrow Wilson's reputation as Governor of New Jersey extended well beyond the eastern seaboard of the United States. To his already considerable reputation as a scholar and university president he had added that of a vigorous and successful state Governor. There was no longer any doubt that he was 'Presidential timber'.

In the winter of 1911 a group of influential Democrats formed themselves around the Presidential candidacy of Woodrow Wilson and, with his consent, lobbied support during the spring and early summer of 1912. When the national party convention of more than 1,000 delegates assembled at Baltimore in Maryland on 25th June, there were two leading contenders for the nomination. One was Wilson, the other James ('Champ') Clark, who had become Speaker of the US House of Representatives in 1911 and was thus a national figure both inside and outside the party. Other contenders came forward, but the main battle was clearly between Clark and Wilson.

At the first ballot of delegates 'Champ' Clark was ahead of Wilson, though a good way short of the required two-thirds majority to secure the party nomination. The Wilson supporters stood firm and the party proceeded to a marathon series of ballots—forty-five in all—before Wilson emerged the victor. He owed his nomination in part to William Jennings Bryan, head of the Nebraska delegation, who at a crucial stage in the balloting switched his vote from Clark to Wilson, bringing most of the Nebraska delegation with him. Bryan had his reward

Left: *Theodore Roosevelt, leader of the 'Bull Moose' Party in the 1912 elections, orating from the verandah of his home*

from Wilson before the year was out.

1912 was a good year for the Democrats, for the Republican Party was split. Roosevelt's successor, President Taft, had proved a disappointment to the Progressive wing of the Republican Party, and in the eyes of many people the reforming zeal of Roosevelt's day had relapsed under Taft into an unadventurous conservatism. By 1912 the quarrel in the party was an open split. When Roosevelt decided to throw his hat into the ring for the Presidential election, there was dismay in the ranks of orthodox and loyal Republicans. Most of them clung to President Taft, who was duly nominated by the Republican convention at Chicago in June. Balked of the party's nomination, Roosevelt and his supporters held their own convention under the banner of the Progressive or 'Bull Moose' Party. The split in the Republican forces was now deep and bitter.

In the campaign Roosevelt displayed much of his earlier magnetism. The contest was really between himself and Wilson, with Taft trailing badly as the election results in November confirmed. Roosevelt fought under the slogan of the 'New Nationalism', an amalgam of patriotism and Mid-Western Progressivism. Wilson's slogan was the 'New Freedom', a phrase intended to sum up his programme of taking government out of the hands of the financiers and big business interests which, he charged, had held the Republican Party in thrall for decades. Government would be returned to the people. The farmer, the small businessman, the patient middle class, the thrifty worker would all benefit from the 'New Freedom'. Wilson's pledge was a shrewd package, designed to appeal to the many factions within the Democratic Party: the farmers of the Mid-West and West who still had Populist sympathies, the working people in the big cities, and the heirs of Jefferson in the rural South.

In November Woodrow Wilson was elected with 6,300,000 votes to Roosevelt's 4,100,000 and Taft's 3,480,000. It was a bitter humiliation for Taft. In the elections to Congress the Democrats also improved their position against the divided Republicans. As President, Wilson would have a Democratic majority of seventy-three in the House of Representatives, and a narrower but workable majority of six in the smaller upper house, the Senate. But before he could get down to the details of his programme for his Presidential term of four years, Woodrow Wilson had the difficult task of forming a cabinet and an administration.

Right: *Inauguration Day, 1913 — Wilson and William Howard Taft*

Chapter 4
Reform–to a Degree

Like every newly-elected President, Wilson quickly found himself besieged by office-seekers. Presidential patronage was still very much a part of the political system, as it had been since President Jackson's day in the 1830s, when the doctrine 'To the victor belong the spoils' was first invoked. Hundreds of top jobs in the Civil Service, the Post Office, and the federal agencies in Washington and throughout the Union were deemed to be in the gift of a newly-elected President, who would turn out the appointees of his predecessor and install his own men, usually in recognition of their party services. During the 20th century, reform of the Civil Service has gradually reduced Presidential patronage, and it is safe to assume that most Presidents have been glad to be rid of this headache.

As the demands mounted, Wilson escaped to Bermuda with his wife and two daughters. In the meantime he commissioned a trusted friend, Colonel Edward House, to cast about for good cabinet material. House, a quiet, civilised, and urbane Texan, had known Wilson for little more than a year, but he had a sincere admiration for the new President. Mutual esteem had grown rapidly between the two men during 1912, and by the end of the year Wilson completely trusted House's judgement and discretion. Colonel House himself later recalled: 'Almost from the first, our minds vibrated in unison.' This friendship and mutual trust had immense consequences in the world of diplomacy during the next few years.

Wilson's cabinet was very much of House's choosing. The most notable appointment was that of William Jennings Bryan as Secretary of State, where he would carry responsibility for the conduct of foreign relations. It was not Wilson's most successful appointment, as events were soon to prove. But in view of Bryan's position as a leading party stalwart with an immense following in the Mid-West and West, not to mention Wilson's personal indebtedness to Bryan for his support at the Democratic

Left: Early victory for the new man in the White House — in October 1913 the Underwood tariff-reduction bill became law

convention, the Nebraskan's claims could not be overlooked. Wilson's other appointments were not particularly distinguished, but this was more a reflection of the paucity of talent in the Democratic Party at the time than a reflection on Wilson's judgement.

In April 1913, within weeks of his inauguration, Wilson personally addressed a joint session of the two Houses of Congress, thus reviving a custom which had not been used since the days of Jefferson, President of the Republic during the first decade of the 19th century. The intention, Wilson told the members of Congress, was to let them see for themselves that the President was a person, not merely a department of the government 'hailing Congress from some isolated island of jealous power'.

In some respects this was shrewd politics. The fathers of the Republic had deliberately separated the President from the legislature, and today that separation is still symbolised by the Capitol looming at one end of Washington's Pennsylvania Avenue with the White House at the other. Geographically and constitutionally, the legislature and the executive office are thus divorced, and the fundamental problem of American government is to achieve some harmony between the two.

But the new President's political shrewdness was matched by many experienced members of Congress; men who were serving in the Senate or the House years before Woodrow Wilson stood for the Governorship of New Jersey. They had no intention of letting the President have an easy ride with his legislative programme. It was inevitable. Congress exists both to check the executive power of the Presidency, and also to represent, in the most literal sense, sectional and minority interests which might be overlooked in the broad overview of Presidential action.

Legislating for the New Freedom

Wilson introduced the first measures of his New Freedom programme soon after his speech to Congress. He began with a bill designed to reduce tariffs, the first blow against the protected industrial giants in America. Although the question of tariffs does not loom large among political issues today, it was one of the liveliest issues, both internally and internationally, in the late 19th and early 20th centuries. In America and in Europe bitter battles were fought within national legislatures on the issue of Protectionism versus Free Trade. The protectionist lobby had powerful arguments on its side: ordinary patriotism, the desire to protect domestic markets from a flood of cheap foreign goods, the need to preserve industries and output vital to the national economy and so to defending the standard of living of the nation, and fin-

ally the usefulness of the tariff as a weapon against those foreign nations which operated tariffs against American goods. The defenders of Free Trade argued that tariffs were self-defeating. As soon as one nation – especially a powerful nation like the United States – installed protective tariffs, smaller nations were bound to follow suit in self-defence. The result was a constriction of world trade, with periodic slumps accompanied by monetary crises as investors and producers suffered the dislocations of the market. There was the further argument that tariffs protected inefficient industries at home, giving no incentive for efficiency in facing foreign competition, and thus operating against the national economic interest.

Woodrow Wilson had already declared himself against high protective tariffs, and he now introduced a legislative measure that would bring down the existing tariff, which averaged 40 per cent on a range of goods, to an average of 29 per cent. More importantly, a large number of products would be placed on the free or unprotected list. These included agricultural machinery, iron and steel products, and many consumer goods such as shoes and clothing.

Needless to say, there was immediate opposition from powerfully-entrenched lobbies in Washington. As the bill proceeded through the House of Representatives, the lobbyists swarmed on Capitol Hill, determined to kill the bill or, failing that, to inflict amendments on it. As Woodrow Wilson himself remarked, Washington was so full of lobbyists that 'a brick couldn't be thrown without hitting one of them'. Senators and Congressmen were bombarded with deputations, petitions, leaflets, and sometimes with veiled threats from powerful interests who could make life extremely difficult for the individual legislator in his home district. President Wilson struck back. On 26th May he denounced the 'industrious and insidious' special interests who were seeking to 'create an artificial opinion and to overcome the interests of the public for private profit'.

Many members of Congress had stock holdings in the affected industries – either directly or indirectly; some in wool and sugar – two major items on the free list – or in cotton and citrus fruits. Strong opposition was encountered in the Senate, therefore, but when Wilson proposed an inquiry on which all Senators would be requested to declare any holdings which might be affected in any way by tariff reductions, opposition declined sharply. By September 1913 the tariff bill had passed through both Houses of Congress and the President's signature brought it on to the statute books. The editor of the London *Nation*

Left: Bryan, Woodrow Wilson's Secretary of State from 1913-15

wrote that this victory raised Wilson 'at a single stage from the man of promise to the man of achievement'.

Another reform on which Woodrow Wilson had set his heart was that of the banking and currency system. The existing system, formed half a century earlier during the Civil War, lacked any coherence or central control. In periods of crisis there was no system for mobilising the banking reserves of the country. Banks operated independently of each other and the overall money supply was not geared in any way to the fluctuating demands of industry, investors, and the public. A bankers' panic in 1907 was still fresh in the public mind, and now that tariffs were to be reduced, the need for stability in the banking and monetary system of the country required urgent attention.

Recommendations were already before Congress when Woodrow Wilson became President. These resulted from the deliberations of a National Monetary Commission which was set up after the 1907 financial panic. Known as the Aldrich Plan (the commission was headed by Senator Nelson W. Aldrich of Rhode Island), these recommendations suggested the setting up of a central bank with fifteen branches in various parts of the country. The central bank, the commission advised, should have the power to issue currency tied to gold and commercial paper. Liabilities would be the responsibility of the central bank, not the government.

The proposals brought vigorous opposition from agrarian and Western interests which regarded them as merely the perpetuation of Wall Street control: the nation's banking system would be in the hands of the same East Coast financiers and gold peddlers who had fought the Populists of the 1890s. As the opposition mounted, Woodrow Wilson appointed another committee to go into the question, but this in turn came up with proposals against a central bank, favouring instead a loose system of reserve banks with no one bank dominant. This satisfied neither Wall Street nor the agrarian interests and by this stage the revolt against Wall Street was headed by William Jennings Bryan, the anti-gold Democrat of 1896. He had powerful support from Senators and Congressmen across the continent for his insistence that the federal government itself should take responsibility for the banking reserves and the issue and supply of money.

Woodrow Wilson recognised the strength of the movement behind Bryan and agreed to the compromise which finally emerged after protracted discussions between the

Right: The pot and the kettle—while the US preaches peace between the nations, racial hatred disfigures American life

Congressional committee and leading bankers. The Federal Reserve Act transferred to the government responsibility for the supply of money. The ultimate responsibility for the level and adjustment of reserves belonged to the new Federal Reserve System of banks operating in all areas of the United States. The new system prevented the concentration of reserves and credit in New York City close to the volatile New York Stock Exchange, it established machinery for the mobilisation of the entire banking reserves of the nation in times of crisis or emergency and, at the same time, it permitted private enterprise banking at the local level. In the opinion of many, the Federal Reserve System was the greatest achievement of Woodrow Wilson's first term as President of the United States.

The President now turned to the problem of regulating industrial combinations. The problem had grown acutely as the combinations grew bigger and began not only to fix the price and level of production in order to maximise profits, but to eliminate competition by obtaining monopoly control of supply and distribution in key industrial processes.

There was already anti-trust legislation on the statute book, notably the Sherman Act of 1890, but this had many loopholes, and crucial passages were ambiguous or obscure. The Act did not define with any precision words like 'combination' and 'trust', or terms like 'restraint of competition'. As a result, corporation lawyers had long discovered how to exploit the 1890 law on behalf of their clients. What was needed now was a severe tightening up of the existing law.

Under the Clayton Anti-trust Bill, sponsored by the chairman of the House of Representatives Judiciary Committee, Henry D. Clayton, many loopholes in the law would be stopped. Such abuses as interlocking directorates in industrial concerns capitalised at $1 million or more, the acquisition of stock holdings tending to lessen competition, and tied contracts and price discriminations tending to assist the creation of monopolies would all be prohibited under the proposed new act.

One major hurdle the bill encountered in Congress involved organised labour in the United States. The American Federation of Labour demanded that trades unions should be exempted from the provisions of anti-trust or monopoly legislation. From the AF of L's point of view unity was strength; competition between rival unions for membership and funds would weaken organised **40** ▷

40 ▷

Left: A gathering of the Ku Klux Klan — disappointingly, in spite of Wilson's generally sympathetic attitude towards civil rights, the persecution of black Americans continued unabated

Urban America

During the Presidency of Woodrow Wilson the United States became for the first time predominantly a nation of city-dwellers. The growth of American cities in this period was closely linked with the industrial boom created by the Great War. And before 1914 the urban population was swelled by the vast tide of immigration, mainly from Central and Eastern Europe (**below:** immigrant family in New York). The size of America's cities began to rival and surpass those of the Old World. By 1920 over 2½ million people were living in Chicago, over 5½ million in New York. The wealth and grandeur of her cities also increased rapidly. New York's fabulous skyline (depicted on the **right** by the artist Jean Negulesco) became world-famous. Still, more than almost any other, American cities offered sharp, sometimes dismaying contrasts. At the foot of their mighty skyscrapers huddled some of the most wretched slums—and slum-dwellers—in the Western world

labour in its dealings with employers. Woodrow Wilson proposed a compromise whereby injunctions against unions in labour disputes were circumscribed. But Samuel Gompers, President of the American Federation of Labour, fought hard, and eventually won vital concessions, so much so that the final bill, according to Missouri Senator James Reed, lacked any teeth at all: 'When the Clayton bill was first written,' declared Reed, 'it was a raging lion with a mouth full of teeth. It has degenerated to a tabby cat with soft gums, a plaintive mew, and an anaemic appearance.'

1914 was the year of mid-term elections to the United States Congress. As they drew closer Wilson was worried about the relations between his administration and the business community. A depression had set in during the autumn of 1913. It continued through the winter and mounted in the spring of 1914. In fact it was a world phenomenon, the result of a tightening of credit in Europe as the Balkan Wars brought fear of general war. If the recession continued in the United States, however, things would go ill for the Democrats in the 1914 Congressional elections. Woodrow Wilson might well lose his slender majority in the Senate, and even in the House if things got worse between April and November.

Making friends with capital

He therefore sought a rapprochement with the business and banking community. The influential financier J. Pierpont Morgan was welcomed to the White House, along with delegations from business and industrial firms. Wilson's Attorney General was instructed to provide help and guidance to large combinations such as the American Telephone and Telegraph Company or the New Haven Railroad as they sought to re-arrange their corporate structure to satisfy the new laws. Some felt that the Justice Department was being altogether too helpful to the trusts, and Progressive elements in the Democratic Party began to feel betrayed. Feelings grew worse when leading bankers and businessmen were appointed to the Federal Reserve Board. When the membership was announced, a leading Progressive observed bitterly that they might well have been appointed by the president of the National City Bank of New York.

Wilson disappointed liberal and Progressive opinion on other issues as the two-year Congressional term drew to a close. Women were still denied the suffrage. To bring it about would require an amendment to the American Constitution. Conservative Southerners in the Democratic Party were bitterly opposed to such a measure. Like many English politicians and statesmen, they felt that women should not become involved with what was so

often a sordid process, best left to the men. It is difficult for us to appreciate this line of reasoning today, though it was put forward in all sincerity by gentlemen at the time. Woman's place, they asserted, was in the home managing the household (and so far as the middle classes were concerned, managing the servants), a job which was more than enough to cope with between bearing children for their husbands.

In fact, Woodrow Wilson shared these views. However, he took refuge in claims of political necessity when women petitioned him for his support. He assured the delegations that there was no earthly hope of getting a bill through Congress. This angered and alienated the suffragettes, and effectively delayed woman suffrage for five years. Only the wartime contribution of women working alongside their menfolk in factories and on war work brought the necessary change of opinion in America, as it did in Britain.

The Negroes were also disappointed by Wilson's inactivity. Segregation between whites and Negroes was commonplace throughout the United States. In the deep South it was maintained by state laws. Elsewhere, segregation was maintained by social habit and convention, not to mention gross disparities of income. In the field of job opportunities, racial discrimination was rife, the common plea of the whites being that Negroes were not sufficiently educated to take on skilled jobs requiring intelligence or reasoning. This was the familiar circular argument of course. Negroes were not suited to educated tasks, therefore society should not trouble to educate them to the task.

Wilson's attitude to Negroes would now strike the modern liberal as deeply conservative. Although he valued the friendship of those few Negroes who had somehow managed to secure an education — men like Booker T. Washington for instance — he was not offended by such practices as segregation in schools, churches, eating places, and transport. As a Southern city, Washington itself bore plenty of witness to such segregation. But this again was a burning political issue, and Woodrow Wilson did not need to ask the white Southern Democrats what their attitude would be to legislation for improving the educational and economic opportunities of the Negro.

On the other hand, Wilson had appealed for Negro support in the 1912 Presidential election, and white liberals and Progressives had campaigned for him with high hopes of securing progress for the Negro should he

Left: The 'woman question' was much in the news during Wilson's first term: suffragette pursues the mouse of male supremacy (top); 'emancipated' women in a New York bar (bottom)

41

be elected. It was natural, therefore, that liberals such as Oswald Garrison Villard, a founder of the National Association for the Advancement of Coloured People, should ask the new President about his legislative plans for Negro advancement. The result was keenly disappointing. Wilson showed general sympathy with the cause, but had no proposals. When Villard and his colleagues produced a plan for the appointment of a National Race Commission, composed of eminent white and Negro leaders to study and report on the whole problem, Wilson was non-committal. Villard pressed, but the President replied that the situation was much too delicate to appoint such a body. What he meant was that Democratic Senators and Congressmen from the deep South—on whom he depended for his majorities in Congress—would so much resent the Commission that the rest of his legislative programme would be endangered. The proposal was dropped.

Thereafter, relations between President Wilson and those articulate liberal spokesmen inside and outside Washington who wanted reform of injustices, cooled markedly. Their ranks included many journalists and educationists. The November 1914 elections brought severe reverses to the Democrats. Their majority in the House dropped from seventy-three to twenty-five. The balance in the Senate remained unchanged, but in state elections the Republicans made impressive gains in the more populous states of the East, in the Mid-West, and in the prairie states. If Woodrow Wilson intended to seek a second four-year term of office in 1916, the outlook was gloomy.

But August 1914 had brought new elements into the political situation. The conflagration which everyone had feared had now burst upon Europe. What should the American attitude be towards the belligerents? Was Germany the aggressor? How should the blame be apportioned between the chief colialist powers, Britain, France, and Germany? How far would the war spread? Could the United States afford to sit back? As head of state and Commander-in-Chief of all American armed forces, Woodrow Wilson could not ignore these questions, nor could he shirk the issues they raised. Moreover, there were many other problems in the sphere of foreign relations, and Wilson was already caught up in them.

Left: Socialist Eugene Debs at a labour convention. Wilson's reformism was spurred on by the existence of a growing body of left-wing support. In 1912 Debs polled over 900,000 votes

Chapter 5
Uneasy Neutrality

When Wilson arrived in the White House in 1913 the most vexatious item on the diplomatic calendar was the Mexican situation. The dictatorship of Porfirio Diaz, which had been hospitable to American investments and interests, had ended with the revolution of 1910-11. Further upheavals in Mexico led to the authoritarian Huerta regime. Woodrow Wilson refused to recognise the new dictatorship, and Mexican-American relations went from bad to worse, culminating in the bombardment and occupation of Vera Cruz by American forces in April 1914. Peace was finally secured by the good offices of Brazil, Chile, and Argentina, but the price of peace was the retirement of Huerta and the appointment of Carranza as President. The United States recognised the new government and other Latin-American nations followed suit.

The rapprochement with Mexico was merely one part of Wilson's general policy of seeking to eliminate Latin-American jealousy and resentment of the United States. Wilson formulated a general policy of goodwill to the larger states on the sub-continent to the south and the smaller states in the Caribbean.

American interest in the Caribbean area had sharpened considerably as a result of the building of a canal across the narrow isthmus of Panama. When Woodrow Wilson came to the Presidency the canal was nearing completion. In an age of imperialism and big navies, when sea power was deemed to be a prime factor in hemispheric power and influence, the importance of the new canal could not be exaggerated. The United States would depend on it to move her fleets in peace and in war between the Atlantic and Pacific oceans.

President Roosevelt's action in securing Panama as an American protectorate had greatly angered the Caribbean countries. It was a classic case of a big and powerful nation imposing its own terms on a small and weak state.

Left: Woodrow Wilson, the officious policeman, takes complaints from the fish — German cartoon mocks the President's concern for the right of neutrals to travel unharmed upon the high seas

45

Roosevelt himself had boasted 'I took Panama'. Some gesture of good will, if not of contriteness, was now required from the United States if the rupture was not to continue. Wilson's policies were therefore wedded to what one historian has termed 'conscience-stricken diplomacy'.

High on the calendar was the keen resentment felt in Colombia, Panama's neighbouring state on the isthmus, at Roosevelt's bullying diplomacy. Colombia's relations with Panama were, of course, vitally affected by Panama's new subservience to American interests. Roosevelt had authorised the payment to Panama of extensive dollar funds as part of the price for acquiring the Panama Canal Zone. Colombia demanded some proportion of the largesse. Accordingly, in 1914, Wilson drafted a treaty with Colombia to meet this demand. The treaty authorised an indemnity of 25 million dollars, allowed Colombia and her citizens the same rights to use the canal as the United States and her citizens, and expressed sincere regrets to the Colombian government on the part of the United States for any past actions which might have marred the relations between the two governments. Ex-President Roosevelt promptly denounced this proposed treaty which soon became bogged down in the Senate. After long delays it was passed in a form which omitted the apology but which admitted the indemnity.

Wilson's diplomacy elsewhere in the Caribbean encountered many setbacks, partly as a result of political instability among the existing regimes and partly as a result of bad appointments by Secretary of State William Jennings Bryan to key diplomatic positions in Nicaragua and the Dominican Republic. Affairs in Haiti were particularly unstable and after several revolutionary uprisings Wilson authorised United States marines to land in July 1915 until a more stable regime was installed. Overall, Wilson's pacifism and good intentions had to be diluted by the overriding importance of protecting American interests in the area as the Panama Canal neared completion in 1914.

In August 1914, in the midst of all this activity, personal tragedy darkened Wilson's life. After a long illness his wife died. Now that she was gone he seemed a broken man. Happily for Wilson's peace of mind, his physician introduced him to a handsome widow, Edith Bolling

Right: Mexican revolutionary general Pancho Villa. In March 1916 Villa raided into New Mexico, killing seventeen US citizens. Wilson despatched a punitive expedition under General Pershing, but Villa proved elusive and the 12,000 American troops south of the border soon became a diplomatic embarrassment. After repeated angry requests from the Mexican government, Wilson withdrew the US force in February 1917

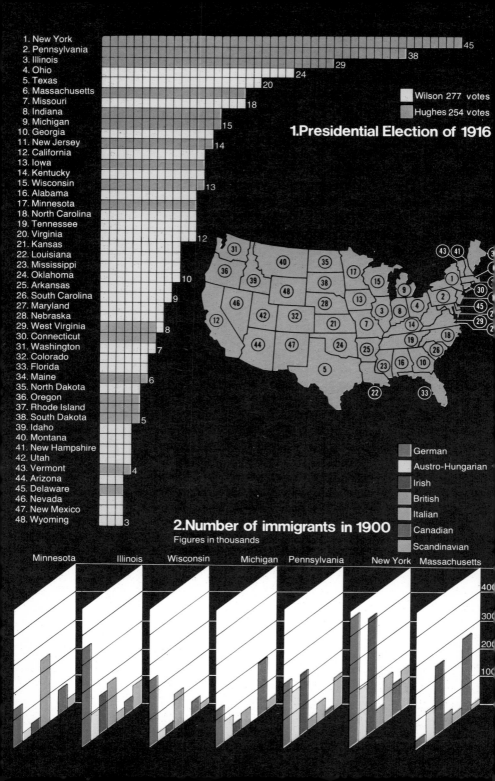

1. New York
2. Pennsylvania
3. Illinois
4. Ohio
5. Texas
6. Massachusetts
7. Missouri
8. Indiana
9. Michigan
10. Georgia
11. New Jersey
12. California
13. Iowa
14. Kentucky
15. Wisconsin
16. Alabama
17. Minnesota
18. North Carolina
19. Tennessee
20. Virginia
21. Kansas
22. Louisiana
23. Mississippi
24. Oklahoma
25. Arkansas
26. South Carolina
27. Maryland
28. Nebraska
29. West Virginia
30. Connecticut
31. Washington
32. Colorado
33. Florida
34. Maine
35. North Dakota
36. Oregon
37. Rhode Island
38. South Dakota
39. Idaho
40. Montana
41. New Hampshire
42. Utah
43. Vermont
44. Arizona
45. Delaware
46. Nevada
47. New Mexico
48. Wyoming

45
38
29
24
20
18
15
14
13
12
10
9
8
7
6
5
4
3

Wilson 277 votes
Hughes 254 votes

1.Presidential Election of 1916

German
Austro-Hungarian
Irish
British
Italian
Canadian
Scandinavian

2.Number of immigrants in 1900
Figures in thousands

Minnesota   Illinois   Wisconsin   Michigan   Pennsylvania   New York   Massachusetts

400
300
200
100

Galt, a gay, conversational woman of patrician background and civilised tastes. The affection between the pair blossomed quickly and they married in December 1915. This was somewhat too soon for staid consciences in Washington society, but it brought stability once more to Wilson's life. The new Mrs Wilson emerged as a formidable woman, very ready to protect her husband from unwelcome visitors, even vetting those suggested by Wilson's aides and assistants. Relations between Wilson's private secretary, Joseph Tumulty, and the new First Lady were at times strained.

But events in Europe and around the world had not waited on personal bereavements and readjustment in the White House. Britain, France, and Russia were now at war with Germany. In the autumn and winter offensives of 1914 the Germans had achieved outstanding victories. On the seas, Britain used her vast navy to blockade Germany in an effort to starve her of supplies. Yet this meant interfering with neutral shipping, including American vessels. Strong notes were issued from the US State Department, for William Jennings Bryan was no particular friend of Britain. As a Nebraskan, he belonged to the heartland of America, where large numbers of German immigrants had settled in the 19th century. His political career had already revealed in good measure that he resented the Anglo-Saxon leanings of the East Coast Establishment in the United States. He held his views with a passionate sense of rectitude and, like the majority of Mid-Western Americans, he was by no means convinced that Germany was the aggressor in 1914.

The German propaganda machine was also very highly organised in the United States when the war broke out. It already had a base, of course, in the German-language newspapers which flourished in many parts of the United States. In New York City there was the influential *Staats-Zeitung*. In Ohio and Wisconsin, in Texas and in the Dakotas, German-Americans were proud of the literature, the history, and the culture of their homeland. They believed in Germany's innocence in 1914. Taken together, these German-Americans made up voting blocks in crucial sections of the national electorate. And 1916 was a Presidential election year.

Woodrow Wilson's policy between 1914 and 1915 was one of strict neutrality. As soon as the war broke out he issued an official proclamation of neutrality and followed

Left: The 'peace election' of 1916. Though Wilson's supporters boasted 'he kept us out of the war', Republican Hughes got significant support from states with large populations of 'hyphenated' Americans, especially German- and Irish-Americans

this up with a personal appeal to all Americans for impartiality of thought as well as of action. Where American interests were directly affected, however, as in the case of British interference with ships proceeding to German ports, Wilson agreed with Bryan's protests.

However, 1915 brought the German submarine menace. In February, attempting to counteract the British blockade, Germany declared the seas around Britain a war zone and warned that all belligerent ships would be sunk. The decree also hinted that neutral ships in the same waters risked being sunk. On 10th February Wilson warned Germany that the destruction of any American vessel or loss of any American lives would be construed as a violation of neutrality and the German government would be held to 'strict accountability'. Germany replied that the British blockade left her with no option but to retaliate in this way. The British policy, she remonstrated, was aimed at starving the German people. William Jennings Bryan accepted the 'starvation' pleas, but other Americans did not. As correspondents and diplomats confirmed, there were ample supplies of food in Germany, and in any case the British blockade was almost a failure.

German folly

Various incidents followed, some involving American shipping, and in March 1915 an American citizen was killed aboard a British steamer. On 7th May newspapers throughout America carried the headline that the British liner *Lusitania* had been sunk by a German submarine near the Irish coast. American public opinion was shocked by what seemed the senseless murder of 1,200 civilian non-combatants. Moreover, among the passengers were 128 Americans. The action of the submarine commander was clearly political folly of the first magnitude. Anger boiled up among ordinary citizens throughout America as the news spread. There were demands for immediate revenge, and if not that, some firm gesture from the American President to show that the murder of innocent Americans could not be tolerated.

Wilson drafted a Note demanding that Germany abandon her policy of 'unrestricted' submarine warfare and make reparation for the loss of American lives. Wilson repeated the American policy of 'strict accountability' for all such actions. In reply the German government claimed that the *Lusitania* was armed (in fact it was not, though it carried a shipment of rifles and ammunition), and that clear prior warnings had been given in statements to American newspapers by the German Embassy in Washington more than a week before the vessel's departure from New York.

Wilson found the German reply unacceptable and drafted another Note demanding specific pledges concerning American shipping and lives. As with the first Note, he passed it to Bryan, his Secretary of State, for signature and delivery to the German Embassy and the German High Command. But Bryan refused to sign. He had signed the first Note with some reluctance, feeling that it discriminated against Germany, making her appear the aggressor on the high seas. A convinced pacifist, Bryan was against any action that might bring America into the war. The second Note, he argued, might well involve a final breach with Germany. As the Note clearly involved a vital matter of policy, Bryan resigned on 7th June 1915. His resignation was promptly accepted. The poor relationship between Wilson and Bryan now came out into the open. The Note was despatched to Germany over the signature of Bryan's successor, Robert Lansing. A third Note went out on 21st July warning that any repetition of these acts would be regarded as 'deliberately unfriendly'. Stripped of diplomatic niceties, America was warning Germany to desist or face war.

The break between William Jennings Bryan and Woodrow Wilson was almost bound to come sooner or later. Bryan deeply resented the way in which the President hardly ever took him into his confidence. Wilson clearly preferred the advice of his chosen aide Colonel Edward House — especially on foreign affairs — and to some degree Bryan's position had become intolerable by mid-1915. Apart from Bryan's pacifism and desire for a policy of strict neutrality, one further cause of the rupture was his loss of face after Wilson's decision to send Colonel House on a vital diplomatic mission to Europe to talk with the heads of government on both sides of the conflict. Wilson wished to know what were the war aims of the belligerents so that he could estimate or surmise how far the conflict was likely to spread and which territories it would affect in the immediate or distant future. Another objective of the House mission was to learn whether the good offices of the United States might be used to mediate and bring the war to an end.

House left for Europe and commuted between London, Paris, and Berlin, talking with the three governments separately, trying to discover what concessions he might obtain from each of them in the interests of securing an end to hostilities. By April 1915, on House's second visit to London, Grey was prepared to agree to end the British blockade in return for Germany's consent to general disarmament. But the sudden news of the sink-

Left: Part of Villa's 'Golden 100', his most loyal followers

ing of the *Lusitania* in May even as these parleys were making some headway, shattered hopes for the present. In June a despondent House left London. Back in Washington, as Notes flew between Germany and the United States, House confessed that he could see no alternative to America being drawn into the war sooner or later.

But the American people were still strongly divided between those who favoured strict neutrality and those who favoured American engagement in the war. We must remember first that neutrality was deeply entrenched in the American mind, particularly where quarrels among the European nation states were concerned. To many Americans such quarrels were merely continuations of earlier dynastic and territorial squabbles which the Europeans had maintained for centuries. It was largely to escape from Europe and its problems that so many Americans had come to the New World. The present war was very largely the fruit of colonial rivalries, of the scramble for Africa and commercial rivalry in the Far East. In Europe statesmen were still thinking in terms of the balance of power—meaning, as George Bernard Shaw was to remark, a balance in their own favour.

The affairs of Europe were not the concern of the American Republic: this was the sincerely-held belief of millions of ordinary Americans. Even if an American President had wished to bring the nation into the war on one side or the other, therefore, he would have to run the gauntlet of public opinion. And should he carry the nation into war—the outcome of which was far from certain—he would carry a dreadful responsibility if he endangered the peace and security of the United States.

Up to late 1915 Woodrow Wilson clung to his policy of neutrality, even though this was intensely unpopular to many articulate spokesmen. One of his chief critics was Theodore Roosevelt, living in vigorous retirement from politics, and urging American preparedness for her inevitable entry into the war. Between 1914 and 1915 Roosevelt wrote a series of articles in the *New York Times* and in weekly magazines urging that the United States should take steps to repair its military weakness by increased production of armaments. America was totally unprepared, Roosevelt argued, if she should suddenly be dragged into the war. Ordinary prudence required that she should not leave herself defenceless.

Woodrow Wilson tried to play down these admonitions. In October 1914 he had genially dismissed such talk as 'good mental exercise' and in his Annual Message to Congress on 8th December he declared, 'We shall not

Right: *Rest and recuperation, 1914-style: American marines take it easy during their successful 'police action' in Vera Cruz*

alter our attitude . . . because some amongst us are nervous and excited.' This did not sweeten relationships between Wilson and the energetic ex-President, and during the next two years the rift was to widen to tragic proportions. Roosevelt had never had a high opinion of Wilson's competence in foreign affairs. The President's stand-pat inactivity angered Roosevelt as the months went by, and he began to organise with friends to force Wilson's hand. In December 1914 a group met in New York City to form a National Security League to urge on Congress and the President a programme of preparedness. The movement quickly gathered pace as veterans' organisations added their support. The sinking of the *Lusitania* gave an immense boost to the movement, and Wilson found it more and more difficult to stem the demand for action.

Calmer waters

Pro-German propaganda in the United States continued. It was being organised very efficiently from the German Embassy, which some observers felt had become more of a propaganda machine than an embassy. There was also increasing evidence of a well-developed spy ring, as well as sabotage in the United States organised by German agents. But from August 1915 the German authorities instructed submarines to avoid sinking liners, following the loss of two more American lives in the British steamer *Arabic*. On 5th October the German government apologised to the US government, offering indemnity for the loss of life on the *Arabic*.

Wilson still hoped to mediate in the European war and Colonel House continued with his missions to Europe. In January 1916 he travelled to London to confer with Grey and Balfour, then on to Paris and Berlin. House had with him a set of proposals for the summoning of a peace conference between the belligerents, with the United States acting as mediator. House won Balfour and Grey to the idea, and on 22nd February the House-Grey Memorandum was published. This stated that President Wilson, 'on hearing from Britain and France that the moment was opportune', would summon a peace conference. Should the Allies accept such a conference and the Germans refuse, then the United States 'would probably enter the war against Germany'.

This brought no comfort to the German High Command. It indicated that the American attitude leaned towards the cause of the Allies. What had happened to the American policy of strict neutrality? It would take too much space to recount in fine detail how the pro-Allied mood had crystallised over a period of more than eighteen months. Certainly incidents other than the sinking

of the *Lusitania* had their effect. Again, the new Secretary of State Robert Lansing was an Anglophile with many English friends. So was Colonel House. The President himself, it should not be overlooked, was proud of his British pedigree—Scotch-Irish on his father's side, English on his mother's. He had many English friends whom he liked and admired. Chief among them was James, Lord Bryce, the English scholar and statesman, who had been a personal friend for many years. Bryce, a leading authority on American history and politics, had written a classic work *The American Commonwealth* which Woodrow Wilson had admired and extolled. When House came to London on his diplomatic missions, it was with Bryce that he communed at length when the formal talks with Balfour and Grey were done. On each occasion he brought President Wilson's personal regards.

Such personal ties of sentiment and mutual regard are easily overlooked when affairs of state are under historical scrutiny. Historians are sometimes apt to rate them fairly lightly. Yet American Presidents are lonely men, especially in times of crisis, and it is at such moments that they particularly miss and long for the easy intimacy of old friendships. If Woodrow Wilson had favoured the German cause in the First World War he would have severed a friendship with his long-time friend James Bryce, whose lectures he had attended and deeply admired as a young graduate at the Johns Hopkins University in 1883, and whom he had welcomed to Princeton on numerous occasions between 1906 and 1910. Bryce had written a good deal on the menace of Prussian militarism in books and articles. Wilson was one of his more avid readers. Bryce had also served on a judicial tribunal in Belgium which investigated Belgian reports of atrocities by German troops on the civilian population. The report made disturbing reading, but its veracity was confirmed by scores of witnesses, by diaries and documents. War always brutalises, and no national army can claim a monopoly of virtue. Nevertheless, the publication of the full report of the Bryce Commission in the United States in 1915 greatly strengthened anti-German feelings.

The House-Grey Memorandum bolstered hopes of a mediated peace, and Wilson promptly endorsed it following the return of Colonel House. Germany, however, remained silent, and even the British agreement had been carefully circumscribed by Grey's proviso that any British promise to attend a conference would require the sanction of the British cabinet after full discussions. Wilson began to lose patience with both sides.

Left: *Colonel Edward M. House, Wilson's roving ambassador to Europe in the years before America entered the war*

American feelings were once again aroused in March 1916 by the *Sussex* affair. The *Sussex*, an unarmed French cross-channel steamer, was torpedoed on 24th March. Among the eighty casualties were several Americans. Secretary of State Lansing was for an immediate severance of diplomatic relations with Germany, but Wilson favoured a more cautious response. Public opinion was so inflamed, however, that spokesmen in Congress demanded vigorous action to make certain that there would be no repetition of such incidents. Lansing's advice finally prevailed, and on 18th April Wilson issued what was nothing less than an ultimatum to Germany. It warned that unless the German government ended its attacks on unarmed passenger and merchant ships, the United States would sever relations. Intense diplomatic activity followed, with Germany seeking to extract from Wilson a similar condition against the Allied blockade of Germany. Wilson refused and remained adamant. Germany pinned a rider to her acceptance, insisting that the United States compel the Allies to observe the 'rules of international law', but Wilson ignored it and accepted the German assurances without the rider.

The American Presidential elections were now only six months away. The campaign for preparedness had continued, with Theodore Roosevelt among its most vigorous spokesmen. Wilson, prompted either by conviction or by electoral prudence — perhaps a mixture of both — gave his assent to a National Defence Act which provided for a rapid expansion of the regular army to 175,000 men, plus a National Guard of 450,000 men, and an Officers Reserve Training Corps. In August a Council of National Defence was established and charged with the task of co-ordinating industry and national resources in a national programme of preparedness. These resources included munitions of war, transport, raw materials, engineering and manufacturing processes, and medicine and surgery. On 7th September a Shipping Act came into force which provided for the building, leasing, or requisition of vessels in time of national emergency.

The Presidential campaign began. The Republican Party had nominated Charles Evans Hughes, an ex-Governor of New York State and a justice of the US Supreme Court. He was a much respected candidate and the Republican Party had almost healed the divisions of earlier campaigns. The Progressive Party still existed, however, and hopefully nominated Theodore Roosevelt

Top, left: *7th May 1915 — the fateful German torpedo depicted streaking towards the defenceless* Lusitania. **Bottom:** *Abandon ship! — over one hundred Americans lost their lives in the tragedy.* **Top, right:** *German medal commemorates the event*

for President at its convention. But Roosevelt declined the nomination and declared his support for Hughes and the Republican Party.

The Democratic Party made peace in America the main item in their campaign. 'He kept us out of the war' was their chief slogan on behalf of President Wilson, and it proved very effective, to some extent cutting the ground from under the feet of the Republican candidate. But the Democrats had a good deal of trouble with the Irish-American and German-American vote over Wilson's clear leanings towards the Allied cause. The Irish-Americans were deeply hostile to any support of England. The Irish troubles were flaring once again in Westminster on the issue of Irish independence. In April 1916 the Irish flag was hoisted on Liberty Hall in Dublin and the bloody Easter rising followed. After the rebellion more than 3,000 Irishmen were arrested and fifteen were executed after secret trials. These events were fully reported in America, and the well-organised Irish immigrants — who had formed much the largest proportion of immigrant Americans during the 19th century and whose political organisations had a firm grip on the vote in many cities — marched and demonstrated against the London government. Needless to say, the German-Americans, also well-organised in areas of German immigration, followed suit and sometimes joined forces with the Irish.

These factors complicated Wilson's electoral strategy for November 1916, and though he travelled widely, with the publicity which naturally accrues to a serving President, the results of the November elections proved uncomfortably close. Wilson gained just over 9 million votes, Hughes 8½ million.

With the results confirmed and Wilson re-elected President for a further term of four years, another diplomatic Note was despatched from Washington on 18th December to the Allied and Central powers. This time the Note did not suggest a peace conference with American mediation, but merely asked the belligerents to state their war aims. It was not a propitious moment for such an initiative. On the Western Front the Allied armies were being reinforced in preparation for a spring offensive. The German army had fallen back to strong defensive positions along the Hindenburg, or Siegfried, Line. But both sides had suffered appalling casualties during the battles of Verdun and the Somme in 1916.

On the Eastern Front, Roumania fell in December 1916 to the combined assaults of the German and Bulgarian forces. Bucharest was taken on 5th December. In Russia, January 1917 brought the first stirrings of the

Left: *1916 — Wilson's platform: peace, prosperity, preparedness*

59

revolution, when ministers were dismissed for supporting constitutional reforms and the Duma (the elected consultative body) was weakened. With the downfall of the Tsar in March, the corrupt regime finally fell and the Duma appointed a provisional government.

These events gravely affected the strategy of the Allied commanders. The position on the Eastern Front was now uncertain. At the same time Germany was over-extended, and heavy losses on the Somme had seriously depleted her reserves and armaments. Small wonder that Wilson's Note asking the belligerents to state their war aims proved fruitless. The German government did publish a statement to all neutral powers expressing her willingness to enter upon peace negotiations, but as she stated no peace terms the Allied powers declined the proposal. On 10th January 1917 a joint reply from the Allies to the United States suggested peace terms which were clearly harsh for the Central Powers.

Once more Wilson began to lose patience with both sides in the war. So far as he was concerned, the House-Grey Memorandum was now dead. Since American attempts at mediation had failed, fresh policies were required. Wilson now believed that the only way forward was to seek a 'peace without victory', and this must be achieved by a league of nations uniting to impose a peace on the belligerents. On 22nd January Wilson delivered a speech to the United States Senate in which he outlined his proposals. They were sincere, idealistic, but somewhat vague so far as concrete proposals were concerned. After setting forward his view that it must be a 'peace without victory', so that neither side would force a peace settlement upon the other with consequent humiliation and resentment, Wilson's voice grew stronger as he warmed to his peroration: 'I am proposing, as it were, that the nations should with one accord adopt the doctrine of President Monroe as the doctrine of the world: that no nation should seek to extend its polity over any other nation or people, but that every people should be left free to determine its own polity, its own way of development, unhindered, unthreatened, unafraid, the little among the great and the powerful.'

Such sentiments were, of course, welcome to everyone, but they were declarations of piety and principle, not concrete proposals for getting the belligerents to a peace conference. The Senators warmly applauded the President. Some remarked afterwards that they had listened to one of the great addresses of modern history. 'It was the greatest message of a century,' observed

Left: A 'blind' American on an 'unarmed' British merchant ship: German sneer at the outcry over the drowning of US passengers

Senator La Follette. 'We have just passed through a very important hour in the life of the world.'

But the war continued. On 1st February Germany resumed her policy of unrestricted submarine warfare. This represented a victory for the military in an internal struggle that had gone on in Germany between the civilian and military elements for more than six months. The military insisted that the positive advantages to Germany outweighed the likely or possible disadvantages. Still anxious to avoid American intervention in the war on the side of the Allies, a German Note assured the United States that she would be permitted to send one ship each week to England, provided the vessel obeyed certain conditions specified by the German government — such ships must be painted with red and white stripes and carry no contraband.

This violation of Germany's earlier *Sussex* pledge precipitated a final break with the United States. On 3rd February the USS *Housatonic* was sunk after a warning. Wilson addressed the Congress on the same day, announcing the severance of diplomatic relations with Germany. Yet he avoided any belligerent utterance in his address. 'We do not desire any hostile conflict with the Imperial German government,' he declared. 'We are the sincere friends of the German people and earnestly desire to remain at peace with the government which speaks for them. We shall not believe that they are hostile to us unless and until we are obliged to believe it.'

Nevertheless, the latest German moves provoked public opinion once again, and military advisers stressed the immediate need for war preparations in case hostilities came. Wilson tried to play down the concern of the military, but quietly agreed to some of their proposals. In Congress the naval appropriations bill was amended to provide for increased construction. The President was also granted powers to take over shipyards and munitions factories in the event of war or national emergency. A conscription bill was formulated and made ready for immediate implementation should it prove necessary.

The pacifist movement in America had not yet given up the ghost, however. With William Jennings Bryan as their most forceful spokesman, peace groups were formed across the nation. They demanded that a war referendum precede any decision for war, and called for a general strike if and when war was declared. But patriots and interventionists were now equally vociferous, and with spokesmen like Theodore Roosevelt issuing continuous streams of pro-war propaganda, the battle for the public mind swung violently between both sides.

Wilson continued to hope for non-involvement. He detested war and shrank from the carnage, brutality,

and senseless loss of life which he knew it entailed. But on 25th February 1917 his hopes were all but ended by the shocking news which reached Washington from London. The British Foreign Office had intercepted and decoded a message sent from the German Foreign Secretary, Alfred Zimmermann, to the German minister in Mexico City. The contents were startling. In the event of Germany being involved in war with the United States, the minister was to propose to the Mexican government an alliance by which Mexico would enter the war against the United States and receive in return 'the lost territories in Texas, New Mexico, and Arizona'. Mexico was also to urge Japan to switch to Germany's side in the conflict. The first action of Wilson and his advisers was, of course, to check the authenticity of the telegram. With Teutonic thoroughness, the German Foreign Office had sent the coded message by three different routes, one of which was the State Department's wire to the German Ambassador in Washington, Bernstorff. This wire was being secretly tapped in London. The State Department had recorded details of the coded wire, therefore, but its experts had not yet cracked the code. London had, however, even though it was very anxious that neither the German nor the American government should know that it was tapping their wires. Since the telegram had also been sent by wireless code direct to Mexico City, a British agent in Mexico was given the task of obtaining a copy of the coded message from the Mexican wire service. It was this copy which the British Foreign Office handed over to the American Secretary of State.

President Wilson received it on 25th February. He was deeply shocked, then angry, with a sense of betrayal. For many months now he had laboured to bring about an honourable peace for Germany. Yet Germany was secretly bribing America's neighbour into war against the United States. The bait of Texas, Arizona, and New Mexico rankled most in Wilson's mind. Any thoughts or illusions about the high-mindedness or integrity of the Imperial German government now vanished. Lansing's private warnings and repeated urgings were now vindicated. Wilson still shrank from the prospect of engaging America in the European war. But now it seemed that his hand was forced. National honour demanded more than another warning Note.

*Left, top: Cartoon points out the two sides of Uncle Sam's neutrality. **Bottom:** Wilson's Republican opponent in the 1916 elections, Charles Evans Hughes, ex-Governor of New York State*

Chapter 6
Towards the Brink

At ten o'clock on the morning of 26th February—the day after Wilson received the details of the Zimmermann telegram—the President's Secretary, Joe Tumulty, telephoned the Capitol to say that the President wished to address both Houses of Congress at one o'clock that afternoon. Permission was granted and the news spread rapidly among the Senators and Congressmen in their offices on Capitol Hill. The President was escorted into the House and began his speech a few minutes after one o'clock.

Wilson had so far withheld news of the Zimmermann telegram. He wished its authenticity to be thoroughly checked out first. Despite the buzz of rumours and the unexpected address to Congress, the President did not call for a declaration of war against Germany. Instead, he requested from the Congress emergency powers in case he needed to act promptly in the face of any sudden threat to national security. Under the Constitution the power to declare war is vested in the Congress, not the President, even though the President will normally give formal utterance to such a declaration, acting through Congress on behalf of the American people. The President stilled the doubts and worries of those Senators and Congressmen who were deeply opposed to war with Germany. 'I am not now,' he stated, 'proposing or contemplating war or any steps that need lead to it. I merely request that you will accord me by your own vote and definite bestowal the means and the authority to safeguard in practice the right of a great people who are at peace and who are desirous of exercising none but the rights of peace.'

In concrete terms, Wilson went on to request powers to supply arms to merchant ships, should this become necessary, together with the necessary monies for improving the national defences both at sea and on the land. Even as the President was speaking, news filtered into the chamber that a German submarine had sunk the Cunard liner *Laconia* with Americans on board. Word passed from mouth to mouth as the President continued.

Left: As war looms, the pacifist spirit runs high in America

At the end of his speech most of the Democrats applauded warmly. The Republicans stood in silence as the President departed from the chamber.

In the debate which followed his request, Congress empowered the President to spend up to $100 million for the purposes he outlined. The national press was mostly for Wilson. On 27th February the influential *New York Times* declared, 'The time and the occasion for action has come. We must defend our people and our seamen in the exercise of their rights or make a cowardly surrender to the power that has forbidden us to exercise them.' America was inching towards war.

The press also carried details of the American casualties on board the *Laconia*. Six American passengers and fourteen crew members had been on board when the liner was torpedoed near the Irish coast on 25th February. An American woman and her daughter were among those who died of exposure. The news was carried alongside President Wilson's address to Congress.

During the next few days the State Department was busy thoroughly checking the authenticity of the Zimmermann telegram. The information passed to President Wilson by Lansing placed the matter beyond doubt. Wilson was duty bound to release it to the press, and on 1st March it erupted in headlines throughout the United States. A cartoonist in the *New York World* portrayed the Zimmermann telegram exploding like a bomb in the hands of the German foreign minister. Not even the sinking of the *Lusitania* affected the American people so deeply as this latest outrage. On the same day Congress voted President Wilson's armed ship bill by 403 to 13.

The German-American press promptly declared the Zimmermann telegram a forgery. It was, stated the New York *Staats Zeitung,* merely the latest effort by the pro-Allied propagandists to foment public feeling against Germany. But the bulk of the press was solidly against Germany in the matter. A typical editorial appeared in the *New York World:* 'Germany has been making war upon the United States for more than two years. It has not been an open and honourable war but a sneaking and despicable war. . . . In all the history of nations there is no other record of such a lying friendship as that which Germany has professed for the United States.'

As if to underline the point, Zimmermann admitted to news reporters on 3rd March that he had sent the telegram to Von Eckhardt, though stressing that his proposal to Mexico was contingent on the United States declaring war on Germany. The bait of three states of

Right: Fears of American unpreparedness — Columbia depicted without 'arms' as the flames of the Great War approach her

ARMLESS

the Federal Union was not referred to. But it almost seemed that Germany had come to expect war with the United States. On 12th March the unarmed SS *Algonquin* was torpedoed. A few days later, three merchant vessels, the *City of Memphis, Illinois,* and *Vigilancia* were sunk with heavy loss of life.

The furore mounted. Theodore Roosevelt roared for war. In the *New York Times* on 20th March he demanded a war declaration by Congress. On the same day the Union League Club of New York held a meeting, attended by 600 Republican leaders and many distinguished citizens, including editors, scholars, and men of letters. They declared in a resolution: 'War now exists by the act of Germany.' Two days later a mass meeting in Madison Square Garden, New York cheered Theodore Roosevelt when he again called for war.

Divided nation

Did this mean that the American nation was now demanding war against Germany? By no means. In the Mid-West and West, and in many areas of the South, the majority were still for peace and neutrality. About twelve members of the Senate still publicly resisted the cry for war. On the Left of the political spectrum, the Socialist leader Eugene V. Debs called on organised labour and all trade unionists to resist the cry for war. To Debs and the American Socialist Party American public opinion was being manipulated by the Wall Street financiers and industrialists who were merely seeking the bigger profits from the huge contracts that would come their way if America went to war. Debs called for a general strike if the Wall Street capitalists persuaded the President into war.

Wilson himself kept his own counsel as the public debate raged. Following the sinking of the three American vessels and the loss of crew members, Wilson called Secretary of State Lansing to the White House. Lansing recorded in his diary: 'For an hour the President and I sat in his study and debated the course of action which should be followed. The President said that he did not see that we could do more than we were doing in the way of protecting our vessels. . . . I argued that war was inevitable, that I had felt so for months, and that the sooner we openly admitted the fact so much stronger our position would be with our own people and before the world. I left the President without a definite impression as to what the decision would be.'

Woodrow Wilson remained silent in the White House. The United States' relationship with Germany was still officially one of armed neutrality: American ships were armed and instructed to defend themselves if attacked.

The only alternative to armed neutrality was war. Wilson decided to talk with his Secretary of the Navy, Josephus Daniels. Daniels wrote in his diary that the President 'wished everything possible done in addition to Armed Guards to protect American shipping. . . . He had been urged to call Congress and to declare war. He still hoped to avoid it and wished no cost and no effort spared to protect shipping.'

On the same day Wilson asked Frank Cobb, editor of the *New York World,* to call on him at the White House. If Cobb's recollections were accurate, Wilson had edged perceptibly towards the final decision. Cobb recalled: 'He said he couldn't see any alternative; that he had tried every way he knew to avoid war. "I think I know what war means," he said, and he added that if there were any possibility of avoiding war he wanted to try it.'

Cobb replied that the President's hand had been forced by Germany; that so far as he could see America could not keep out of the war.

That same night Lansing drafted a memorandum for the President, reviewing the arguments for and against joining the war. If war was now inevitable, then the sooner America joined in the better. The Allied cause had suffered gravely on the Eastern Front through uncertainties following the Russian Revolution and the new provisional government under Kerensky. American participation in the war would give encouragement to the Russian government, besides strengthening the hand of many people inside Germany who clearly wanted the war brought to an end by an armistice or some peace agreement. The principal effect must be to shorten the war. Finally, America would have a positive say in the peace negotiations and a post-war settlement in Europe only if she committed herself to the conflict now.

Wilson had called a cabinet meeting for the following day; it proved to be one of the most fateful in the history of the Republic. Wilson entered the Cabinet Room apparently relaxed, even genial. After dealing with one or two domestic issues, he announced that he desired the cabinet's views on relations with Germany and the course which should be pursued. He said that from a practical point of view he could not see what more could be done to safeguard American vessels, beyond arming them as at present, unless the United States declared war on Germany or declared that a state of war now existed. The formal power to do this lay with Congress, under the

Top left: British Punch *taunts Wilson's pacifism — cartoon suggests that the war-like eagle should take the place of the gentle dove in the face of German provocation. **Bottom**: Uncle Sam reveals a Wilson even more patient in adversity than Job*

Constitution, of course. But what did members of the cabinet advise? What should the President recommend to Congress? The President's cabinet proved unanimous in favour of war. In a quiet, calm voice, the President said, 'Well, gentlemen, I think that there is no doubt as to what your advice is. I thank you.'

Wilson did not announce his own opinion or intentions. The cabinet meeting ended. In the next few days Washington correspondents swarmed around the government departments as rumours of impending decisions multiplied, feeding upon each other. Still Wilson kept his own counsel. But on 23rd March he summoned a meeting of the Council of National Defence. They met in closed session. Next day the American minister to Belgium was instructed to withdraw from Belgian territory, together with members of his mission. At home the navy and marine corps were increased in strength, and some units of the National Guard—equivalent to British territorial brigades—were mobilised. On 29th March a new army bill was introduced, increasing the regular army to war strength and authorising the conscription of 500,000 men by 'selective draft'.

By 31st March there was no doubting that war fever was spreading. Newspapers carried reports of public meetings throughout the United States calling for war. In Philadelphia's historic Independence Square many thousands paraded in support of a declaration of war. In Chicago, heartland of Mid-Western isolationist tendencies, a mass meeting was addressed by the State Governor, followed by a public procession urging war. Other meetings took place, from New Hampshire in the North-East to Colorado in the South-West. Some observers found evidence that people in the rural areas and in the prairie states were still for keeping out of the war, but their voices were not heard in the mounting clamour.

The decision to recommend war to the Congress now rested with the American President. It would be difficult to overstate the agony of spirit which Woodrow Wilson was now enduring. Colonel Edward House was at the President's side in Washington, and noted in his diary that on 27th March Wilson was complaining of headaches and feeling unwell. He discussed with House whether his best action would be to ask Congress to declare war on Germany, or to declare that a state of war already existed, coupled with the request to Congress for the means to carry on the war. As the two men communed, House noted the President's agony and wrote in

Right: 'Crazy Horse' Wilson on the 'phone—German view of the diplomatic Notes sent to Imperial Germany by the President

70

his diary, 'The President said he did not believe he was fitted for the Presidency under such conditions.' House agreed: 'I thought he was too refined, too civilised, too intellectual, too cultivated not to see the incongruity and absurdity of war. It needs a man of coarser fibre and one less a philosopher than the President to conduct a brutal, vigorous, and successful war.'

Wilson had already informed the Congress that he wished to address both Houses on 2nd April. This required the Congress to convene early in extraordinary session. On 31st March he buried himself in his office, preparing his address. The Chief Clerk at the White House noted in his diary, 'The President is sitting before his own little typewriting machine, and slowly, but accurately and neatly, typing a message which will probably be his greatest State paper.'

On Sunday, 1st April the President took a long drive with his wife in the afternoon air. After dinner he worked again in his study, completing his address around ten o'clock. Secretary of State Lansing called at the White House next morning, and went over the War Message he had been instructed to draft. Congress assembled at noon. As this was the first session of the Sixty-fifth Congress, there were procedural arrangements to be completed before the President could be invited to address the two Houses. The afternoon passed, and the President sat talking with Lansing and Colonel House. Lansing felt that the President should have an armed guard on his way to the Capitol, but Wilson dismissed the idea. Nevertheless, Lansing insisted on providing an escort of cavalry. There were reports of scuffles on Capitol Hill between pacifist demonstrators and members of Congress seeking to enter their offices. One of the demonstrators exchanged blows with Senator Henry Cabot Lodge, a leading spokesman for war. Shortly after eight pm Mrs Wilson, with Colonel House, left for the Capitol. The President followed a few minutes later, accompanied by Joseph Tumulty, an army aide, and an escort of cavalry. In the packed chamber of the House of Representatives members of the House and the Senate waited.

The President advises

The President entered a minute or two after eight-thirty. He began his address in a matter of fact, almost conversational tone: 'I have called the Congress into extraordinary session because there are serious, very serious, choices of policy to be made, and made immediately, which it was neither right nor constitutionally permissible that I should assume the responsibility of making.' Wilson went on to review the events and executive decisions since publication of the Zimmermann tele-

gram. He outlined the policy of armed neutrality which he had earlier thought sufficient and practicable, but which had proved ineffectual against attacks on American vessels. Then the President came to the crucial part of his address: 'With a profound sense of the solemn and even tragical character of the step I am taking and of the grave responsibilities which it involves, but in un-hesitating obedience to what I deem my constitutional duty, I advise that the Congress declare the recent course of the Imperial German government to be in fact nothing less than war against the government and people of the United States; that it formally accept the status of bellig-erent which has thus been thrust upon it; and that it take immediate steps not only to put the country in a more thorough state of defence but also to exert all its power and employ all its resources to bring the govern-ment of the German Empire to terms and end the war.'

Even before he had finished the sentence, the packed chamber erupted into wild cheering, the entire Congress on its feet, the Chief Justice of the United States vigor-ously leading the applause which followed.

The President continued. He stressed that Americans had no quarrel with the German people – merely with the Imperial government which had thrust its policies upon them. 'The world must be made safe for democracy,' he said, in a phrase which soon entered the history books. The American people would fight 'without rancour, and without selfish object, seeking nothing for ourselves, but what we shall wish to share with all free peoples'. Woodrow Wilson brought his address to a close with a moving peroration: 'To such a task we can dedicate our lives and our fortunes, everything that we are and every-thing that we have, with the pride of those who know that the day has come when America is privileged to spend her blood and her might for the principles that gave her birth and happiness and the peace which she has treasur-ed. God helping her, she can do no other.'

The President had spoken for just over half an hour. At the end, members of the Congress rose again, cheering wildly. Wilson left the Capitol to return along Pennsyl-vania Avenue to the White House. The news had already been relayed to the crowd lining either side of the streets. They cheered and clapped as the President's carriage drove by.

Back in the White House, Wilson sat down in the Cabinet Room and turned to Tumulty. 'Think what it is they are applauding,' he said. 'My message today was a message of death for our young men. How strange it

Left: 1917 – brought back home to meet a much greater crisis, American troops parade on their return from service in Mexico

73

seems to applaud that.' The President steeled himself as he talked on: 'In carrying on the war we will be obliged to do certain unusual things, things that will interfere with the lives and habits of our people. . . . Our life, therefore, until this thing is over, and God only knows when it will be over, will be full of tragedy and heartaches.'

And bitter criticism besides. Away in the West, in the German-American townships of Wisconsin and Nebraska, many citizens deplored the President's call for war, even though, constitutionally, the decision for war had yet to be taken by the United States Congress. On 4th April the Senate debated the measure placed before them by the President. The debate went on all day and into the night as most of the Senators wished to have a say in the historic debate. Almost all the speeches were in favour of the President, though a handful of Senators from the prairie states and the West were passionately against war. A Nebraskan Senator denounced the decision as a conspiracy engineered by the Wall Street capitalists. 'We are going into war upon the command of gold,' he declared in a speech full of bitterness. 'We are about to put the dollar sign upon the American flag.' The old sectional animosities of the Populist era appeared briefly once again. But when the vote was taken eighty-two were in favour, only six against.

The debate in the House followed, and continued to 6th April. The vote was 373 to fifty. The Speaker of the House of Representatives promptly signed the resolution. The Vice-President added his signature as chairman of the Senate, and a messenger left the Capitol immediately for the White House. Woodrow Wilson signed it within the hour. The United States was now at war with Germany. An official proclamation followed and signals were despatched to American diplomatic missions, to army units, and to all naval vessels.

Left: *Washington, April 1917 — on the eve of war President Wilson addresses a joint session of the United States Congress*

I WANT Y
FOR U.S. AR

Chapter 7
America at War

American intervention in the war came at a vital time for the Allied cause. The French armies were suffering badly in the Aisne and Champagne areas on the Western Front. Nivelle, Commander-in-Chief of the northern armies, suffered a disastrous defeat in his attempt to capture Laon. Mutiny broke out among the French troops as their morale crumbled, and many units of the French army were paralysed. The British offensive in Flanders after June gained little ground and suffered heavy casualties. Heavy rain in August brought on the muddy hell of Passchendaele. On the Eastern Front the Russian armies were weakened by the internal troubles in Russia as Bolsheviks and Mensheviks struggled for control of the government, dividing the loyalties of the military. Russia was lost as an ally after the November Revolution, when the Bolsheviks emerged as victors and Lenin formulated the policies that were to take Russia out of the war by a separate peace treaty in March 1918.

America had only about 200,000 men in her army when she entered the war, but this was gradually expanded to a total of 4 million by the end of the conflict. Selective service provided over $2\frac{3}{4}$ million of these. A total of forty-two divisions went to France during the war, each division containing 1,000 officers and about 27,000 men. About 1,400,000 American troops saw combat duty.

This was a major contribution to the Allied cause. In May 1917 General John Pershing was appointed Commander of the American Expeditionary Force (AEF). Conscripting and training the expanded army took some weeks, but by 26th June the first American units were landing in France. Pershing's orders were that the American troops would co-operate with the Allied force in military operations against the enemy, but it was stated that US forces must be regarded by the Allies as a 'distinct and separate component of the combined forces, the identity of which must be preserved'.

Left: Before the end of the First World War the United States had recruited some four million men and women into her armed services. Next page: US troops embarking at Southampton

AMERICANS ALL!

HONOR ROLL

Du Bois
Smith
O'Brien
Cejka
Haucke
Pappandrikopolous
Andrassi
Villotto
Levy
Turovich
Kowalski
Chriczanevicz
Knutson
Gonzales

Victory Liberty Loan

**don't waste food
while others starve!**

UNITED STATES FOOD ADMINISTRATION

Allied commanders initially objected to this direction, but Pershing insisted — as he was instructed to do by Washington — and won Allied consent for a separate American sector of the Western Front, east of Verdun. In September Pershing established his headquarters at Chaumont and on 21st October American troops relieved French units in the Toul sector. At that moment activity was quiet on this sector of the front, but American troops were now face to face with German soldiers and soon the two forces were engaged in combat.

In Washington Wilson had meanwhile put into effect the special powers which Congress had granted to the President for the duration of the war. Under the general supervision of the Council for National Defence, the President set up a series of boards for the mobilisation of America's industrial, agricultural, and manpower resources. Congress quickly passed the appropriations for the immense change required to place the economy on a war footing. Initially there were inevitable dislocations. For a short time the US railroad system almost broke down under the impact of troop movements. Ordinary passenger lines became chaotic as the routing of both troops and military material claimed priority. On 26th December the government took over the railroads and operated the national network as one system, paying the different railroad companies compensation meanwhile. This particular exercise cost the US taxpayer $714 million.

The War Industries Board mobilised the nation's industrial resources. After some reorganisation, it was placed under the control of Bernard M. Baruch, one of Winston Churchill's closest American friends. The board was given wide powers in determining priorities for war production, for taking over and converting industrial plants, for fixing prices, and for purchasing. More than 30,000 articles came under the control of the War Industries Board. Standardisation of product was imposed in order to eliminate waste and increase efficiency in production. Thus the available colours on typewriter ribbons were reduced from 150 to five, pocket knives from 6,000 variants to 144. Even the manufacture of corsets was controlled and new regulations released 8,000 tons of steel annually for war production from the corset industry alone.

A Food and Fuel Control Act, effective for the duration of the war, gave the President power to make regulations for conserving food protection and to control the distribution of both food and fuel. Herbert Hoover, a future

Far left, top and bottom: Propaganda designed for the home front. Left: Hauling down an offending statue of 'Germania'

President of the United States, was appointed Food Administrator and given the twofold task of increasing food production and decreasing ordinary civilian consumption by the elimination of waste. Hoover was given an array of special powers and achieved a brilliant success in persuading the American people to cut down on food consumption and to eliminate waste. Hoover's appeals were, of course, bolstered by appeals to patriotism on behalf of the Allied soldiers fighting in France, but even allowing for this, the American people showed a remarkable willingness to accept war restrictions on such staples as bread and meat. 'Wheatless Mondays' and 'Meatless Tuesdays' became a common experience for most of the nation.

Fuel and power were conserved by daylight saving and the banning of electric displays. Exports and imports were placed under a strict licensing system. A Trading With The Enemy Act of October 1917 prohibited commerce with enemy nations or their associated powers. Censorship was imposed on mails and materials passing between the United States and any foreign nation. The exigencies of war encouraged Congress to pass the Eighteenth Amendment to the Constitution, prohibiting the manufacture, sale, or transportation of alcoholic liquors throughout the United States. 'Prohibition', as the new Amendment came to be known, was to have profound effects in the post-war era and eventually proved unworkable, with its consequent repeal in 1933. Another less than popular measure was the War Revenue Act of 3rd October 1917, which made income tax the chief source of revenue for the war. Here was one war measure which post-war administrations found it necessary – or convenient – to maintain after the war.

Public opinion was mobilised in a variety of ways. A Committee on Public Information, under the direction of George Creel, organised the production and distribution of millions of pamphlets, books, lectures, and addresses designed to strengthen the national will. Truth was often a hostage to reasons of state as professors 'established' that the Germans had always been a depraved people. The new motion picture industry showed propaganda films, and any evidence of German brutality was portrayed luridly, the message of the silent screen reinforced by the rhetoric of the captions. In the schools history was rapidly slanted to portray Allied soldiery as – figuratively-speaking – knights in shining armour; the 'Hun' as a predatory monster, dripping blood.

This manipulation of the public mind was not to the taste of the austere, white-haired man in the White

Right: 'Shape up or . . . .!' – victim of wartime super-patriotism

House. Now in his early sixties, Woodrow Wilson was showing the strain of his high office. His lean frame had the beginnings of a stoop. The rimless spectacles preserved the appearance of the scholar. His cheeks showed the first signs of that cadaverousness which the world saw at Paris at the war's end.

Domestic difficulties

His worries were manifold. The political storm over the Prohibition Amendment rocked the halls of Congress and reverberated in the White House, as the well-organised lobbies of the liquor trade descended on Washington. The cause of female suffrage had not died with the war; indeed, women's war work strengthened the suffragettes' case that women should have a say in the choosing of elected representatives. Congress had rejected the Women's Suffrage Bill of 1915, but the state of Montana had returned a female member of Congress in the following year. Straining under the immense Presidential burden of American involvement in the war, Wilson sought to avoid the issue, urging that it was a matter for the states themselves to attend to, not one for the Federal government. This was only partly true, constitutionally speaking. State laws regulated the grant of the franchise, but the Federal Constitution could—if it was amended—specifically prohibit the denial of the franchise to citizens by reason of their sex—just as it had already prohibited denial by reason of race or religion. An amendment to the Constitution remained the goal of the suffragette movement.

The race problem also persisted. The great expansion of the administration brought many Southern Democrats to positions of power in Washington. Many of Wilson's appointees to boards and departments practised segregation between white and Negro Federal employees. The President could not spare the time or the energy to do anything positive about the situation beyond deploring it privately.

The Russian Revolution provided a serious complication for Wilson's diplomacy both before and after America's entrance into the war. Initially he was prepared to welcome the provisional government of March 1917. Prompted partly by the enthusiasm of Colonel House and of Secretary of State Lansing, Wilson's first conclusions were that the March Revolution effectively killed any possibility of an alliance between the Russian nobility and bureaucracy on the one hand, and Imperial Germany on the other. This suited the plans of the Entente. Moreover, since the provisional government declared its

Left: Steel and muscle—building the 'arsenal of democracy'

violent opposition to imperialism, American and Russian policies were to some extent congruent.

Wilson thus shared the attitude of many liberals in the United States that the end of the Tsarist regime helped to purify the Allied cause, ridding it of the stigma of reactionary associations. At a Cabinet meeting on 20th March 1917 Wilson spoke of 'the glorious act of the Russians'. By 2nd April he spoke with even greater warmth: 'Does not every American feel that assurance has been added to our hope for the future peace of the world by the wonderful and heartening things that have been happening within the last few weeks in Russia? . . . The autocracy that crowns the summit of her political structure . . . has been shaken off and the great, generous Russian people have been added in all their naïve majesty to the forces that fight for freedom in the world. . . . Here is a fit partner for a League of Honour.'

The Russians did not have a monopoly of naïvities. Before long events forced Wilson, Lansing, and Colonel House to revise their judgement of the new regime. In April 1917 Lenin and other Bolshevik leaders arrived in Petrograd from Switzerland. In July the Bolsheviks attempted an unsuccessful coup and Lenin fled to Finland. But the Kerensky government which followed was precarious in the face of growing privations among the mass of the Russian people. The effects of the Revolution and of the war against Germany combined to bring on a weariness and restlessness which the Kerensky government could not contain. November brought another revolution and the flight of Kerensky. At the head of the new regime were Lenin, Trotsky, and Stalin. The Bolsheviks were in power. Russian policies were now based on the tenets of militant Communism.

Wilson clung to his vision of a liberal Russian Republic. His aspirations included a formal understanding with the new republic so that the two powers could rid Europe not only of German autocracy but of imperialism generally. But Lenin's pronouncement against liberalism and capitalism soon cast doubt on the likelihood of such an alliance. Lenin held that a republican government did not mean the end of bourgeois rule over the workers. Bolshevist ideology dismissed all faith in democratic procedures. In his writings Lenin clearly regarded the European war as a struggle between rival capitalist camps, and insisted that the capitalism of the Allies was no less odious than that of the Central Powers.

Dispatches from the American Ambassador in Russia showed that the early hopes of Wilson and his advisers were misguided. Lenin's ultimate aims were clearly to

Right: *US landgirl, 1917—college co-ed down on the farm*

destroy capitalism in one final socialist revolution. Wilson's policy therefore required careful appraisement as the war continued. Meanwhile, Russian troops continued to fight against the common enemy on the Eastern Front and American troops arrived on the Western Front.

The conduct of the war was now Woodrow Wilson's most pressing concern. His mind still sought the means for limiting the conflict and bringing the war to a conclusion, but strategic problems on the battlefields in France, as well as naval operations on the high seas, also demanded their share of the President's attention in his role — constitutional rather than practical — as Commander-in-Chief of the nation's armed forces.

The Navy Department was performing admirably in its greatly-expanded building programme. Secretary Daniels — assisted by young Franklin Delano Roosevelt in the office of Assistant Secretary — responded vigorously to some alarming news from London concerning Allied shipping losses. Woodrow Wilson despatched Rear Admiral Sims to confer with Jellicoe, First Lord of the Admiralty. Sims reported to Washington that the German U-boat menace had so increased and was proving so deadly that without prompt American assistance Allied shipping would be all but driven from the seas before the year's end, and Britain would be starved into surrender. Sims urged the Allies to adopt the convoy system, so that armed destroyers could escort the merchantmen. There was strong opposition to the plan from merchant seamen, who preferred to take their chances individually on the broad Atlantic, rather than help, as they thought, to form a massive target for prowling U-boats. But American insistence prevailed and losses declined markedly thereafter. Between April and November 1917, Allied shipping losses per month declined from 881 million tons to 289 million tons. The sharply-accelerated shipbuilding programme in the United States largely accounted for the much improved situation.

American land forces were now engaged in active combat in the West, but on the Eastern Front the new Soviet government disengaged from the war by concluding the Treaty of Brest-Litovsk. The Russian negotiations with Germany began in December 1917, and as they progressed Germany was able to transfer hundreds of thousands of soldiers to the Western Front, where the Americans were concentrated. The German High Command was preparing a major offensive for spring 1918, and the additional troops gave them numerical superiority along the Western Front. More American troops were rushed from train-

Top, right: *New York police recruits, 1918. Women took over the men's peacetime jobs.* ***Bottom:*** *And the men enlisted in the army*

88

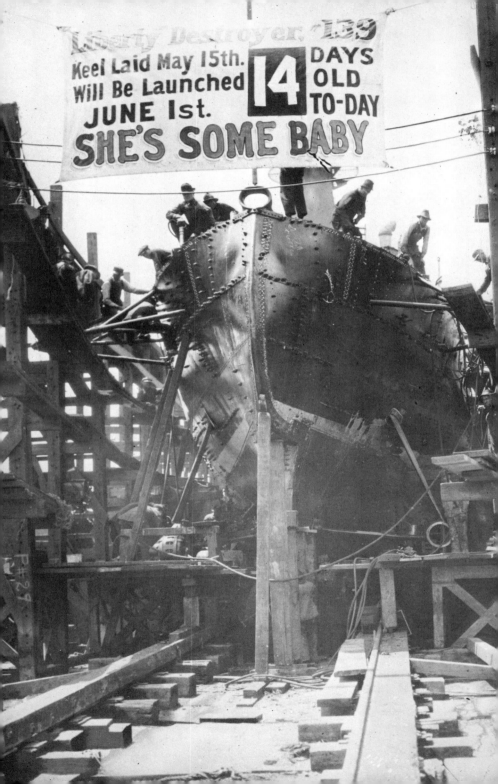

Liberty Destroyer 139
Keel Laid May 15th.
Will Be Launched **14** DAYS OLD
JUNE 1st. TO-DAY
SHE'S SOME BABY

ing units to France. Between March and October 1918, 1¾ million American troops were landed in France. In the opinion of the German commander in the field, von Ludendorff, American intervention became the decisive factor in the war.

When Germany's offensive arrived in late March 1918 her armies achieved spectacular early successes against the British and French lines. With these tactical reverses, the Allied military command repeated their request that American troops be placed under a unified High Command. Pershing agreed and American troops were placed under the command of General Foch, who distributed the fresh American reserves among the battle-weary French and British divisions. Between April and July American troops were in action in almost all parts of the Western Front. As help continued to arrive from America the tide of the battle turned. The German drive on Paris was halted, then turned back.

Woodrow Wilson took a close personal interest in the conduct of the war, especially the supply of manpower and material. It was his overall responsibility to ensure that American armies in the field were well-armed and adequately supplied. He was equally determined that there would be no corrupt profiteering from the war, and Herbert Hoover personally testified to the President's zeal for financial integrity in all departments. He also proved a great administrator, showing speed in evaluating problems and an excellent ability to delegate work in order to retain time and energy for the larger decisions of government and diplomacy.

Framing the Fourteen Points

Wilson had not forgotten his quest for peace and a durable post-war settlement. He set up a group of academics and specialists to study the problem and by January 1918 he was discussing their completed report with Colonel House. An earlier attempt by the Allied governments meeting in Paris had failed to produce an agreed statement of war aims. The situation was made more urgent by the actions of the new Soviet regime, which was already publishing the texts of secret treaties concluded by the Allies. The Bolsheviks declared them to be proof of evil imperialist designs.

The President addressed Congress on 8th January 1918. His speech included a document soon to become widely known as the 'Fourteen Points'. Wilson listed the points as the only possible programme for peace from the American standpoint. They were (in abbreviated form) as follows:

Left: Defeating the submarine in the shipyards of America

91

1. Open covenants of peace, openly arrived at.
2. Absolute freedom of navigation upon the seas.
3. Removal, so far as possible, of all economic barriers to trade.
4. National armaments to be reduced to the lowest point consistent with domestic safety.
5. An open-minded and impartial adjustment of all colonial claims, based upon the principle that the interests of the population concerned must have equal weight with the equitable claims of the government claiming the title.
6. Evacuation by Germany of all Russian territory.
7. Evacuation and restoration of Belgian territory.
8. Evacuation and restoration of French territory, and the return to France of Alsace-Lorraine.
9. Readjustment of the Italian frontiers along lines of nationality.
10. The peoples of Austria-Hungary to be given the opportunity of autonomous development.
11. Evacuation and restoration of Roumania, Serbia, and Montenegro, free access to the sea for Serbia, and international guarantees of the political and economic independence and territorial integrity of the Balkan countries.
12. Nationalities under the Ottoman Empire to be given free opportunity for autonomous development, and free passage through the Dardanelles to be guaranteed for ships of all nations.
13. Establishment of an independent Poland, with free and secure access to the sea.
14. A general association of nations to be formed under specific covenants to afford mutual guarantees of political independence and territorial integrity for great and small states alike.

Most of the Fourteen Points involved questions of territorial adjustment to repair the ravages of enemy occupation. The last point, however, bore witness to Wilson's increasing concern to provide some international peace-keeping machinery when hostilities were done, so that the peace might be a lasting one. For the world community, the Fourteenth Point was thus the most important, even though the other points could – and did – provide plenty of arguments among the nations whose interests were directly or indirectly affected by them.

The deeper significance of Wilson's address on the Fourteen Points was to commit the United States to a positive involvement in the post-war settlement. The importance of this step can be grasped by recalling that it abrogated the principles which had guided American

Right: US troops in action during the Meuse-Argonne offensive

foreign policy for almost a century. Wilson's stand reflected in part a growing American concern at events in Russia. Point 6, concerning the evacuation of Russian territory, was the subject of much discussion between Wilson and his advisers. By January 1918 Wilson and Colonel House had little reason to doubt the attitude of the Bolsheviks towards liberal democracy but House cautioned Wilson to hold out the hand of friendship or at the very least to show sympathy for the Russian people in occupied territory. This was not the time for an assault on the Bolshevik government. The war was not yet won and it was too early to say whether Bolshevism was a temporary manifestation or something which could have grave implications for future peace and harmony in the world. But Wilson and his advisers were equally concerned that the socialist ideologies which underpinned the Russian Revolution should not be imported to the American domestic scene. More immediately, however, the Fourteen Points reflected Wilson's awareness of the overtures Russia was then making towards Germany, and which were to result in the Treaty of Brest-Litovsk on 3rd March. Wilson's address was not intended so much as an international charter for ratification by governments as a diplomatic move to meet these developments and to bolster Allied morale in the light of events in Russia and on the Eastern Front.

There were aspects of the Fourteen Points which the Allied governments in Europe did not entirely endorse, and they accepted them reluctantly, with reservations. The German leaders meanwhile pinned their hopes on the spring offensive in a final bid to end the war on terms favourable to themselves. German victories on the Somme followed in March/April and the Allies were driven back for about thirty miles, with heavy casualties. Yet strategically, the Germans could not hope for victory. With the vast military potential of the United States now under Allied command, and the huge increases in American troop movements between April and August, the final issue was placed beyond doubt. By August the end of the war was in sight. By October German deserters at the front were numbered in hundreds of thousands. On 4th November mutiny broke out among German sailors at Kiel and quickly spread to the Baltic Sea ports. On 6th November Germany's leaders telegraphed Foch, asking permission to send delegates to secure an armistice. Foch's terms were unconditional surrender. The Germans accepted and an armistice was signed on 11th November at five am. Hostilities ceased at eleven am.

Left: *115,000 US soldiers lost their lives during the eighteen months of America's participation in the First World War*

Chapter 8
Peace without Victory

One week before the Armistice was signed, the United States was once more in the throes of the mid-term Congressional elections. Woodrow Wilson still had two years to complete of his second Presidential term, but on 5th November 1918 the electorate went to the polls to elect a new House of Representatives and one-third of the Senate. The Republicans made considerable gains in the election, winning fifty seats in the House and two in the Senate. President Wilson thus lost his Democratic majority in the House, and the Republicans were effectively in control of the Congress.

The election left much bitterness. Wilson had appealed to the electorate to return Democratic majorities so that his position should be strengthened at the peace conference which must inevitably follow the war. Republicans resented this partisan appeal, which appeared to offend against the agreement between the parties that the war should not be brought into the election, lest it divide the nation. When Wilson announced on 18th November that he intended going to the peace conference himself, Republicans were even more incensed. Again they felt the President was planning to make party capital out of national interests.

A further storm broke out when the President announced his team for Paris. They were Colonel House, Secretary of State Lansing, the American Chief-of-Staff General Tasker Bliss, and the diplomat Henry White, ex-Ambassador to France. Of these, only White could be termed a Republican, and no member of the United States Senate was included in the American team. This latter neglect proved to be a tragic blunder on Wilson's part. In the eyes of many, he had insulted the Senate, which under the Federal Constitution was allotted an advisory role in the field of foreign policy.

Wilson sailed for Europe on 4th December aboard the *George Washington*. Mrs Wilson accompanied her husband, and Walter Page, the retiring US Ambassador

Left: 'Hail the conquering hero' : with Poincaré in Paris.

in London, was aboard together with his successor, John W. Davis. Secretary of State Lansing and Henry White were with the party, as well as the French and Italian Ambassadors in Washington.

On 13th December French destroyers escorted the ship into the port of Brest where Generals Tasker Bliss and Pershing came aboard. Mrs Wilson recorded in her diary that on the way to Brest station crowds lined the streets shouting 'Vive Vil-s-on!' Poincaré, the President of France, had sent his own train to bring Wilson to Paris, and it reached the capital next day towards mid-morning. President and Madame Poincaré, the French Cabinet, and American Embassy officials greeted the American President and his wife. The procession moved off in open carriages, through the Arc de Triomphe (as a special gesture to the American President) and down the Champs Elysées, with the Garde Republicaine for escort.

An elegant Paris mansion at 28 Rue de Monceau was placed at the disposal of the Wilsons, and after lunch at the Elysée Palace and two or three days of official greetings and entertainment, Wilson made a round of visits to American war-wounded and American army units in the area. Then there were preliminary meetings with the large American delegation to the Paris conference, including scores of officials from the State Department, together with legal specialists and other experts from Washington.

Christmas brought a brief interlude, and on 26th December the President and Mrs Wilson made a visit to London. The purpose was declaredly social and fraternal between heads of state, and King George was host to the visitors during their brief stay. However, informal talks were arranged with Lloyd George and Foreign Office officials in order to compare the approaches of the two leaders to the coming peace conference. Lloyd George was engrossed with the British general election, which returned him to power as President Wilson arrived, and these preliminary talks were not markedly successful. The personal relationship between the two men was not of the best, though this was more a matter of different temperaments and lack of intimacy than of animosity. 'I have never been quite certain of his real attitude toward this country,' Lloyd George wrote at this time. Apart from this, the brief preliminary discussions disclosed that the British and American attitudes towards the peace treaty and post-war settlement diverged in some respects. These differences were to become more evident when the discussions began at Versailles.

Left: Germany wonders what to expect from the victors: revenge and punishment on a monstrous scale — or Wilsonian mercy?

The peace conference opened on 12th January 1919. It was perhaps the most impressive diplomatic gathering in history, with the plenipotentiaries of twenty-seven nations present. Principal among them were the 'Big Four' — Woodrow Wilson, Lloyd George, Georges Clemenceau for France, and Vittorio Orlando for Italy. These four men eventually held the inner ring during the discussions and deliberations, although the first sessions began with a larger 'Council of Ten'. Other nations, great and small, ringed the four great powers, all of them enemies of Germany or her allies, or nations which had severed diplomatic relations with Germany, including five Latin-American states.

It could reasonably be said that President Wilson was the only one of the Big Four who had no narrow national self-interest to serve. He came as a peacemaker, seeking a settlement which would above all be durable, even if this meant sacrificing strict notions of justice here and there. The tasks facing the conference were enormous, with a host of territorial problems concerning minorities and boundaries to be solved. But the principal question concerned Germany and her possessions, and the reparations she was to pay to those who had suffered.

Clemenceau presided, seventy-eight years old, acclaimed the Father of Victory by his countrymen, and determined that French interests should not be sacrificed. After all, the spoliation and desecrations of the war had taken place very largely upon French soil. German reparations must take note of this fact. Italy, Belgium, and the Netherlands too had strong claims: their lands had also suffered.

President Wilson's main aim was that the conference should accept his Fourteen Points as the basis for all discussions, but this scheme soon ran into difficulties, both procedural and substantive. Lloyd George had no intention of allowing Germany 'freedom of the seas' in any post-war settlement. Indeed, he wished Germany to be deprived of any fleet which might challenge British supremacy in European waters. Other nations placed their priorities on territorial settlements. The idea for a League of Nations to guarantee the peace also met with difficulties. Wilson argued that the League idea was essential to the peace negotiations, and must be an integral part of the settlement. The Europeans felt that discussion on the League should follow and even be treated separately from the vexed question of reparations and territorial settlements. On 25th January, however, the plenary session of the conference voted to in-

Right: *Particularly interesting is the shift in the balance of monetary power: the New World becomes the creditor of the Old*

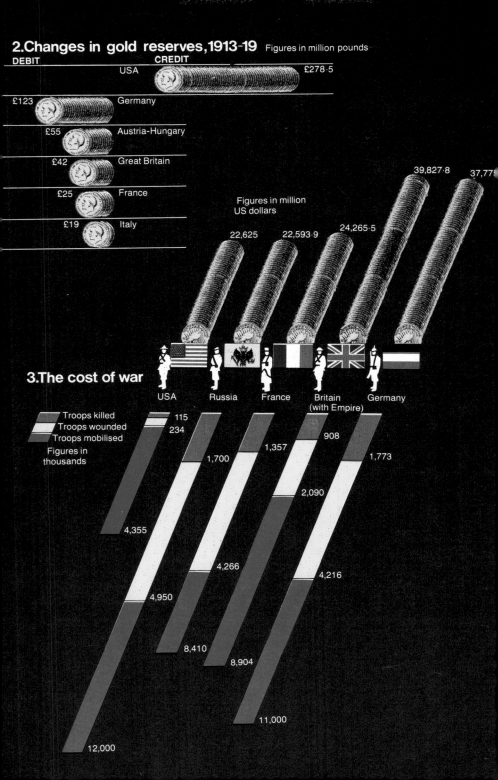

2. Changes in gold reserves, 1913-19   Figures in million pounds

DEBIT   CREDIT

USA   £278·5

£123   Germany

£55   Austria-Hungary

£42   Great Britain

£25   France

£19   Italy

Figures in million
US dollars

22,625   22,593·9   24,265·5   39,827·8   37,775

3. The cost of war

USA   Russia   France   Britain   Germany
                                 (with Empire)

Troops killed
Troops wounded
Troops mobilised
Figures in
thousands

115
234

1,700

1,357

908

1,773

2,090

4,355

4,266

4,216

4,950

8,410

8,904

11,000

12,000

clude the League in the settlement. A commission was set up, presided over by Wilson, to work out a draft covenant for the proposed League. One of the American delegates, David Hunter Miller, and Britain's Lord Robert Cecil were invited to produce drafts, and Wilson himself also set to work to produce one. On 3rd February Wilson presented to the conference a draft which combined Cecil's and David Miller's suggestions with his own, and this was published to the world on 14th February.

Opposition at home

Wilson now made a quick trip home to secure support for the idea of a League of Nations, as well as to attend to constitutional duties awaiting him in Washington. If America was to be a member of the League, public support must be obtained, and Wilson's visit was aimed at persuading leading members of Congress to support his proposals. But the President found virulent opposition to his plans. At a dinner party with members of the House and Senate committees on foreign affairs, he met open scepticism and a battery of questions.

There was no doubting that Wilson's slight to the Senate, by ignoring that august body in the make-up of his party for Paris, was already costing him dear. Again, his partisan appeal to the electorate in the 1918 elections still rankled with the Republican leaders. Wilson's chief opponent on the League plan was Senator Henry Cabot Lodge, the Republican chairman of the Senate Foreign Relations Committee and one of the most influential members of his party. But at least Wilson was spared further criticism from his other long-time opponent on foreign policy. Theodore Roosevelt died on 6th January 1919 just as the nations were gathering at Paris.

Wilson made a further tactical blunder during his short visit to the United States. The Senate was in session, and on this major item of foreign policy the President would have done well to take the draft Covenant to the Senate, asking for their advice and comments. After all, the Covenant was the most important and far-reaching proposal in the realm of foreign policy for almost a century. Even though opposition might be found among the ranks of Senators — as Wilson already knew — it would have been politic, even in an ordinary tactical sense, to allow the Senators to have their say as the elected representatives of the people. Instead, the President chose to seek public support over the heads of the Senators before holding informal meetings with the committees of Congress at a White House dinner.

Sharp criticism of the Paris negotiations also came from the radical and liberal Left. Socialists like Eugene

Debs had hoped that Wilson would seek some sort of fusion with Leninist values in the Paris settlement. Left liberals, gathered around influential journals such as the *Nation* and the *New Republic,* were also angered that Wilson had already made concessions to the French and had utterly failed to unite with those European democratic socialists who aimed to keep Lenin within the democratic camp. The new Soviet constitution of July 1918 ended any hopes of a fusion of Russian and American policies. The Bolshevik Party was now the Communist Party, and on 2nd March 1919 the Third International set Russian Communism on the path of world revolution. A rapprochement between the United States and the Soviet Union was now beyond all possibility.

The President was not without some allies at home, including eminent scholars and men of letters who had been urging a world League to Enforce Peace for more than three years. He also had the support of ex-President Taft, now the only living ex-President, and a Republican to boot. Taft publicly endorsed the President's draft proposals and urged the Senate to support them unanimously. But violent opposition was already growing in the Senate, and before Wilson returned to Paris Senator Lodge had organised a 'Round Robin' which rejected the League in the form proposed by Wilson, and opposed further consideration of the matter until after the peace settlement.

The 'Round Robin' was signed by thirty-seven Republican Senators and two Senators-elect. Lodge's principal objection to the Covenant centred on Article 10 of the document. This would commit the United States to assist the proposed League in guaranteeing the territorial integrity of all member nations. Lodge argued that this would mean an international army, with American troops forming part of it. America would thus be inextricably involved in disputes involving the territorial integrity and political independence of every nation on earth. Lodge felt that the draft was 'loose, involved, and full of dangers' for American interests. The Covenant must be discussed separately and independently of the peace settlement at Paris. On 4th March Wilson publicly defended the Covenant, insisting once again that it was an integral part of any lasting peace settlement; that a peace treaty without such an instrument simply would not last.

The President returned to Paris in mid-March. The other heads of delegations had already returned, following the brief adjournment after the opening sessions. The conference now faced the difficult question of German

Left: *Place de la Concorde, December 1918 — Parisians welcome the US President. Wilson's popularity in Europe was immense*

reparations. The French presented a bill of particulars which included among other things steep demands on Germany for destruction of French land and property, and the creation of a buffer state on the Rhineland, or the imposition of an Allied army of occupation there. Bitter arguments followed. Wilson's Fourteen Points receded rapidly as crude revenge and national selfishness replaced the pious pronouncements of the inaugural sessions of the conference. France clearly wanted security after the ravages she had suffered, but other nations regarded her demands as totally selfish. Orlando, anxious not to be outdone by Clemenceau, the 'tiger' of French politics, pressed Italy's demands. These centred on portions of lower Austria, where Italy sought a strategic boundary for the Brenner Pass. Italy also demanded the port of Fiume, near the head of the Adriatic.

Wilson grew angry as Clemenceau pushed the French demands. The continued strain, and no doubt mounting disillusionment, affected his health, and on 3rd April he fell ill. A few days later reports were circulating that the President had ordered the *George Washington* to Brest again to take him home. France scaled down her demands and agreed to a compromise suggestion by Wilson for a terminable occupation of Germany coupled with an Anglo-American treaty to protect France against any future attack by Germany. The US Senate later declined to pass the proposed treaty. However, France did receive Alsace-Lorraine and the coalfields of the Saar valley, the latter under a League of Nations mandate for a period of fifteen years.

The Italian, Belgian, Polish, and Japanese demands still had to be considered, and Wilson's disillusionment and weariness grew as the sessions went on. After much wrangling, agreed settlements were fixed. On 7th May the Treaty of Versailles was passed to the German authorities. They signed in the Hall of Mirrors on 28th June. Germany now faced punitive damages and the dismemberment of her empire.

Wilson returned promptly to Washington. He was exhausted, but at least the Covenant had been included in the Versailles treaty. His dream of a League of Nations to keep the peace, with the United States a key member, now required the sanction of the US Senate. Wilson was about to face his severest test.

Right: Versailles, June 1919—straining for a glimpse of the historic spectacle. **Next page:** Signing the Treaty of Versailles

Chapter 9
Lost Cause

Debate was already under way when he arrived in Washington. Opposition to the League of Nations had grown as details of the settlement imposed on Germany were given in newspapers. German-Americans were incensed at the terms of the Versailles treaty. Italian-Americans were angry that Italy's claim to Fiume had been denied. More generally, the public was concerned that membership of the League of Nations would commit the United States to a continuing role in the affairs of Europe and to peace-keeping tasks around the globe. Inside the Senate a group known as the 'Irreconcilables' had gathered around the leadership of Senator Borah of Idaho. Henry Cabot Lodge belonged in spirit to this group, which numbered about twelve and was wholly opposed to the treaty, even though he was nominally for amendments and reservations to the treaty, rather than outright rejection. Outside the hard core of opposition was a much larger, fairly fluid group of moderates whose attitude, more or less, was 'wait and see' rather than a definite 'yes' or 'no'. On the Democratic side, the President could count on support from most of his party but he lacked any clear overall majority for his proposals.

As chairman of the Foreign Relations Committee, Henry Cabot Lodge was in a powerful position to influence the terms of discussion and debate in the Senate. He was also a shrewd tactician, and knew that it might be more politic to amend the proposals out of existence rather than declare a flat rejection of the League as Senator Borah and the hard core of Irreconcilables insisted. The fact that the Covenant was an integral part of the Versailles peace treaty meant that the Senate could not reject the League without also rejecting the treaty, thus delaying American acceptance of the peace which public opinion desperately wanted. Lodge's tactic was therefore to produce a list of 'Reservations' — fourteen in all, an unhappy, if fortuitous echo of Wilson's Fourteen Points. Whether Lodge's actions can be disentangled from per-

Left: Cartoon suggests that Wilson is straining the capacities of the little dove of peace with his League of Nations scheme

sonal animosity to Wilson and party political motives must remain conjectural, though in March 1919 Lodge wrote to a fellow Republican Senator, 'My first duty is to keep the Republican Party in the Senate together.' As the summer of 1919 drew on, party politics and personal prejudices on both sides gathered a bitter harvest.

Some of Lodge's Reservations concerned points of detail and interpretation, but their main burden was to question American acceptance of the controversial Article 10 of the Covenant. By July it became clear that the Lodge Reservations were gaining considerable support among Senators as well as outside the Congress. Wilson therefore invited members of the Foreign Relations Committee to meet him again to discuss their objections and reservations. When he addressed the committee on 19th August, he stood firm on Article 10, remarking, 'It seems to me the very backbone of the whole Covenant. Without it the League would be hardly more than an influential debating society.'

Appealing to the people

At the end of August Wilson told his wife that he intended to take his message directly to the people. He would travel across the country for a month or more, addressing meetings, asking the public to support him on the matter now before the Senate. The President's personal physician was deeply opposed to the idea. He observed candidly that he did not think the President could draw further on his strength without risking a breakdown.

Wilson replied that he felt it was his duty to carry out the proposed trip. 'If the treaty is not ratified by the Senate,' he remarked, 'the war will have been fought in vain, and the world will be thrown into chaos. I promised our soldiers, when I asked them to take up arms, that it was a war to end wars. . . . I must go.'

As Dr Grayson had feared, President Wilson began to show signs of acute exhaustion after two weeks of mass meetings. He was suffering from severe headaches, but tried to make light of them as the enthusiasm of the crowds carried him along. From Seattle on the Pacific Coast, the train headed south through Oregon to California, with five major speeches in the San Francisco area alone, on top of more than thirty speeches he had already delivered in twenty-five different cities. The

Left: After the Paris Peace Conference Wilson returns to the United States to the welcome of cheering crowds. But his championship of the League of Nations scheme was to put his popularity among the American people to its severest test

exacting schedule mounted as requests continued to reach the President's secretary. From Los Angeles the train headed East again, to Salt Lake City and Utah. Mrs Wilson and Dr Grayson were alarmed to find the President's coat soaked through with perspiration after these speeches. Even after a change of clothes at the end of the day, he was soon wet through again. At Pueblo in Colorado, on 25th September, he no longer tried to pretend that he was not ill, but still he mustered his strength to make one of the longest speeches on his tour. That night his health collapsed, and by next morning he was an invalid. Still the President tried to insist that he must continue with his speeches, but Dr Grayson and Mrs Wilson could see from his face, haggard, utterly spent, that this was now out of the question. The rest of the tour was cancelled and the train returned to Washington.

Wilson wandered like a ghost in the White House, unable to work because of the excruciating pains in his head. A few days later he rallied slightly and read a chapter of the Bible to his wife — his life-long practice — before retiring to bed. On 2nd October he suffered a stroke which paralysed the left side of his body. One arm and one leg were useless. The brain appeared to be undamaged, but Wilson was never to recover.

The United States now faced a crisis of leadership. The President continued to send messages and instructions from his office, but he was unable to appear in public. The fight for the treaty continued on Capitol Hill. Lodge's Reservations were voted down in the Senate by a combination of Democrats and moderate Republicans. But Lodge was far from beaten by this vote. Outright acceptance of the treaty by the Senate would require a two-thirds vote in favour, and this the Democrats could not muster. There was a clear need for compromise to break the deadlock. The Democrats in Congress were despondent and confused now that their leader was crippled in the White House. The Republicans, on the other hand, were well marshalled by Cabot Lodge and the Republican leaders in the Senate.

No olive branch

Senator Hitchcock of Nebraska, a chief spokesman for the Democratic Senators, visited President Wilson and urged that some compromise was necessary to break the deadlock and to avoid the possibility of rejection by the Senate. His mission was a delicate one, as the President

Right: Wilson prepares to argue his case for the League before the American people. ***Far right, top:*** Senator William E.Borah, leader of the 'Irreconcilable' opposition to Wilson's treaty. ***Bottom:*** A less intransigent, but powerful opponent, Chairman of the Foreign Relations Committee Henry Cabot Lodge

was still adamant on reservations to the treaty, and Dr Grayson insisted that he must not be excited. But Hitchcock felt compelled to suggest a compromise.

'Let Lodge compromise,' the President said from his invalid chair.

'Well, of course, he must compromise also,' Hitchcock replied, 'but we might well hold out the olive branch.'

'Let Lodge hold out the olive branch,' the President retorted. That seemed the end of the matter, and Hitchcock returned gloomily to his fellow Democrats on Capitol Hill.

In the resulting debate, the Democrats voted against Lodge's Reservations, acting on the instructions conveyed from the White House. When the Democrats in turn introduced the treaty with some minor interpretative reservations drafted by Hitchcock, the Republicans in the Senate proved equally loyal to their side, and the treaty failed to obtain a majority. The Senate adjourned.

In December moderate Republicans tried to persuade Lodge to modify his original reservations. Hitchcock also made moves to secure some form of agreement with Lodge and the Republicans, but the Irreconcilables in the Senate flatly opposed any move to meet the Democrats half way. Borah and his colleagues made threatening noises when Lodge edged towards a compromise. Yet public sentiment was now demanding that the politicians produce a solution to the deadlock, and early in January 1920 a bi-partisan conference of Senators began meeting to achieve a compromise. Some progress was achieved, but once again Article 10 proved the sticking point: Borah and his supporters refused to involve the United States in an international commitment, under the authority of the League of Nations, for peace-keeping operations. In a stormy meeting with Lodge, Borah demanded no concessions to the Democrats. Next day he wrote to Lodge declaring that he and his supporters would leave the party and go to the electors on the issue if Lodge did not accede. This threat stopped Lodge in his tracks. November 1920 would bring the Presidential and Congressional elections. A split in the party would ruin the Republicans' chances. At the end of January Lodge admitted that the conference was a failure.

The invalid in the White House remained intransigent. Some further efforts were made in February and March to effect a compromise, but these came to nothing. On a vote in the Senate on 19th March, many Democrats abandoned Wilson and the Versailles treaty was rejected. When Wilson's secretary Joseph Tumulty brought him the result of the Senate vote his only comment was, 'They have shamed us in the eyes of the world'.

Right: *A bitter press campaign was waged against the treaty*

The New
REPUBLIC

Published Weekly

Saturday May 24th 1919

This Is Not Peace

Americans would be fools if they permitted themselves now to be embroiled in a system of European alliances. America promised to underwrite a stable peace. Mr. Wilson has failed. The peace cannot last. America should withdraw from all commitments which would impair her freedom of action.

Whitman, Emerson and the New Poetry
by EMERSON GRANT SUTCLIFFE

Communist Hungary
by H. N. BRAILSFORD

Harry Hawker
by FRANCIS HACKETT

FIFTEEN CENTS A COPY

FIVE DOLLARS A YEAR

VOL. XIX NO. 238

Published by the Republic Publishing Company, Inc., 421 West 21st Street, New York, N. Y. Entered as Second Class matter, November 6, 1914, at the Post Office at New York, N. Y., under the act of March 3, 1879.

June brought the party conventions for the Presidential election. The Democrats nominated Governor James M. Cox of Ohio for President and Franklin D. Roosevelt of New York for Vice-President. The party platform endorsed the Versailles treaty and the League of Nations, but with the important proviso that it was not opposed to 'any reservations making clearer or more specific the obligations of the United States to the League'.

The Republicans nominated Senator Warren G. Harding of Ohio for President and Governor Calvin Coolidge of Massachusetts for Vice-President. The party platform rejected the Covenant of the League of Nations, but made some gesture to public opinion by endorsing a vague commitment to 'an agreement among the nations to preserve the peace of the world'. In the November elections Harding gained the Presidency, defeating Cox by more than 7 million votes.

Woodrow Wilson's Presidency would last until 4th March 1921, when the newly-elected President would take the oath of office. During the final months of his office President Wilson was closely protected by his wife, who barred the way to all visitors, whatever their station. Documents too were vetted by Mrs Wilson before presentation, and for all practical purposes the office was supervised by her during the final six months. President Wilson could still converse, but his mind was weakening. He planned to write a book on his retirement from the Presidency, and before he left the White House he typed out a dedication of the book to his wife. But the book was never written.

In July 1921 both Houses of Congress passed a joint resolution terminating the war with Germany and reserving to the United States any rights secured by the Versailles treaty. Separate peace treaties were concluded with Germany, Austria, and Hungary later that year. President Harding had already put America on the path of isolationism. 'We seek no part in directing the destinies of the world,' he declared in his inaugural address. America had entered the Jazz Age.

The Wilsons lived in Washington in retirement. Woodrow Wilson took no further part in public affairs, though at intervals during the two years after his retirement European statesmen visiting Washington called to pay their respects—Clemenceau, Lloyd George, Lord Robert Cecil. On 3rd February 1924 Woodrow Wilson died at his home. As news of his death spread around Washington, people gathered outside the silent house. Many knelt in prayer. Woodrow Wilson was buried in the crypt of the National Cathedral in Washington three days later.

Left: *'Refusing to give the lady a seat'—cartoon chastises the leaders of the Senatorial opposition to the Versailles treaty*

The Man,
the Statesman

Woodrow Wilson was a moralist before he was a politician. He also possessed the vision and perspectives of the scholar. These qualities did not make for ultimate success in the crude exchanges of democratic politics. By nature reserved and withdrawn, Wilson cared little for the false bonhomie of vote-catching, even though his well-stocked mind gave him a rare eloquence. He could move audiences to tears with passionate utterance, just as he could deflate an opponent when speech-making demanded it. The youthful years of debating equipped him well for such tasks.

He sought power in order to achieve the things he believed in. As an astute student of government, he grasped early the fundamental truth of democratic politics that idealism without power condemns the individual to frustration or despair. He sought power therefore, not for its own sake, but in order to effect changes in society. As a reforming Governor of New Jersey, he had many successes and some failures in attacking political corruption. As President of the United States during his first term, he did much to achieve the new freedoms he had promised the American people. But the war in Europe presented problems which no American President – and no other national leader – could solve. As the conflagration spread, affecting other nations, Woodrow Wilson strove hard to preserve American neutrality, partly because he did not wish the conflict to involve yet another nation, partly because of a basic American reluctance to become involved in the quarrels of the Old World – quarrels in which America had no part; but most of all, perhaps, because of his deep personal horror of what war would bring to the people he led.

But despite his own pacifist leanings, his Christian conscience ultimately convinced him that it would be morally wrong for America to stand idly by as Europe tore itself to pieces. America had a duty to intervene, and as he became convinced that Germany's war leaders

Left: A sick and disappointed man. Woodrow Wilson on the day his successor, Warren G. Harding, was inaugurated President

119

presented a fundamental challenge to the liberal and democratic ideals he shared with his fellow Americans, he finally accepted that duty to intervene.

Fortunately for liberal democracy, the American Congress and the nation supported the President. When the American arsenals were placed behind the Allied cause, the result of the war was no longer in doubt. Even so, Woodrow Wilson addressed himself to the problems of the peace much sooner, and with a much greater commitment, than any other head of state. Again, with the historian's perspective and the analytical insights of a political scientist, Wilson understood well enough that pious hopes and public promises to adjure war would not prevent future conflicts. Peace-keeping machinery, backed by corporate sanctions in one form or another, would alone preserve the peace. His dream was for a League of Nations dedicated to keeping the peace and committed to the protection of smaller or weaker states should their territorial integrity be violated by more powerful neighbours. In Paris Wilson strove hard to realise his dream. The Versailles treaty was not to his liking: greed and motives of revenge seemed to him the chief characteristics of the settlement imposed on Germany. But at least the Covenant of the League survived, and he brought it back to America desperately anxious to secure the endorsement of the Congress and a commitment from the American people. He failed, and the story of his failure was one of the major tragedies of this century. If he had not failed, and if he had lived to carry on his policies or commend them to a successor, the Second World War might well have been avoided — though it is profitless now to speculate on the matter.

Many historians would attribute Wilson's failure to his personal stubbornness, his unwillingness to compromise, his failure to assess the political forces ranged against him in 1920, his failure to recognise that politics — especially democratic politics — is always the art of the possible, and that personal ideals must sometimes yield to political necessity. But we must allow that by 1920 he was an invalid. He had suffered a major stroke, his mind was less agile, his judgement certainly impaired. He was sick, exhausted, indeed a broken man. Nor would it be just to attribute the failure of Wilson's cause to the man's personal shortcomings. The statesman Jan Smuts said after the Paris peace conference: 'It was not Wilson who failed. . . . It was the human spirit itself that failed at Paris.'

Top right: February 1924 — mourners gather outside Wilson's home at the news of his death. *Bottom:* The funeral procession

Chronology of Events

1856	**28th December:** birth of Woodrow Wilson in Staunton, Virginia.
1861 -5	Civil War between North and South.
1875	**September:** entered College of New Jersey at Princeton.
1879	**September:** entered law school at University of Virginia.
1882	Opened law office in Atlanta, Georgia.
1883	**September:** entered Johns Hopkins University.
1885	**June 24th:** married Ellen Axson.
1885	Appointed professor at Bryn Mawr College.
1888	Appointed professor at Wesleyan University.
1890	Appointed professor of Jurisprudence at Princeton.
1902	**August 1st:** appointed president of Princeton.
1908	Beginning of the graduate school controversy.
1910	**November:** elected Governor of New Jersey.
1912	**2nd July:** nominated for the Presidency by the Democratic convention in Baltimore.
	4th November: elected President of the United States.
1913	**3rd October:** Underwood-Simmons tariff law signed by Wilson — his first legislative success.
	23rd December: Wilson signs Federal Reserve Act.
1914	**21st April:** occupation of Vera Cruz by US forces.
	July, August: outbreak of First World War.
	6th August: death of Mrs Wilson
1915	**7th May:** sinking of the *Lusitania*.
	13th May: first of the diplomatic Notes to Germany relating to the *Lusitania* incident.
	18th December: Wilson marries Mrs Edith Bolling Galt.
1916	**March:** raid by Pancho Villa at Columbus, New Mexico. A punitive expedition despatched under Pershing.
	7th November: re-elected to Presidency.
1917	**31st January:** Germany announces unrestricted submarine warfare.
	3rd February: United States severs diplomatic relations with Germany.
	6th April: Wilson proclaims state of war with Germany.
1918	**8th January:** Wilson's Fourteen Points proclaimed.
	12th October: Germany promises to accept Fourteen Points.
	11th November: Armistice with Germany.
1919	**18th January:** opening of the Paris Peace Conference.
	28th June: peace treaty, including the League Covenant, signed in Paris.
	10th July: peace treaty laid before the Senate.
	3rd-26th September: Wilson tours the Western states to rouse support for the League. Collapses in Pueblo, Colorado from over-strain.
	18th November: Wilson refuses to accept a compromise over the treaty.
1920	**20th March:** treaty returned by the Senate to the President having failed to get the necessary two-thirds vote.
1921	**4th March:** Wilson leaves the White House; succeeded by Republican Warren G. Harding.
1924	**3rd February:** death of Woodrow Wilson.

Top: The first Mrs Wilson, Ellen Axson (left); the second Mrs Wilson, Edith Bolling Galt (centre); Wilson's birthplace in Staunton, Va. (right). Centre: Advertisement for US War bonds (left); call for draft registration in September 1918 (centre); a patriotic tableau featuring flags of America and her new allies (right). Bottom: German propaganda attacks short-shrift given pacifists in war-time America (left); John Pershing, commander of the American Expeditionary Force (centre); delighted GIs arriving home from France (right)

Index of main people, places, and events

Author's suggestions for further reading

Woodrow Wilson has been well served by biographers, and there is an embarrassment of riches on almost all aspects of his life and career. The standard work for many years was R.S. Baker's *Woodrow Wilson, Life and Letters* (8 vols.; New York, 1927-39); but this is now replaced by a definitive multi-volume work by Arthur S.Link; *Wilson* (6 vols. to date; Princeton and London 1947-   ).
For those who require something less ambitious than Link's monumental work in progress, general works on Wilson include John M.Blum's *Woodrow Wilson and the Politics of Morality* (Boston, 1956); E. David Cronon's *The Political Thought of Woodrow Wilson* (New York, 1965); John A.Garraty, *Woodrow Wilson* (New York, 1956). Particular aspects of Wilson's life and thought are covered by the following (all currently in print): H.W. Bragdon, *Woodrow Wilson, the Academic Years* (Harvard); D.W. Hirst, *Woodrow Wilson, Reform Governor* (Rutgers); Arthur S. Link, *Woodrow Wilson and the Progressive Era, 1910-1917* (New York, 1954); T.A.Bailey, *Woodrow Wilson and the Lost Peace* (New York, 1944); T.A. Bailey, *Woodrow Wilson and the Great Betrayal* (New York, 1945); Herbert Hoover, *The Ordeal of Woodrow Wilson* (London, 1958); N.Gordon Levin, *Woodrow Wilson and World Politics* (London, 1958). A more intimate glimpse of Woodrow Wilson is provided by Edith Bolling Wilson, *Memoirs of Mrs Woodrow Wilson* (London, 1939), a gossipy work which may be contrasted with the slightly more critical Joseph B.Tumulty, *Woodrow Wilson As I Knew Him* (New York, 1921), which in turn may be supplemented by John M. Blum's *Joe Tumulty and the Wilson Era* (Boston, 1951). Adulatory sketches are presented in E.B.Alsop's symposium *The Greatness of Woodrow Wilson, 1856-1956* (New York, 1956). Wilson's final years are treated in Gene Smith's *When the Cheering Stopped: Woodrow Wilson's Last Years* (New York, 1965).

Library of the Twentieth Century will include the following titles:

Russia in Revolt
David Floyd
The Second Reich
Harold Kurtz
The Anarchists
Roderick Kedward
Suffragettes International
Trevor Lloyd
War by Time-Table
A. J. P. Taylor
Death of a Generation
Alistair Horne
Suicide of the Empires
Alan Clark
Twilight of the Habsburgs
Z. A. B. Zeman
Early Aviation
Sir Robert Saundby
Birth of the Movies
D. J. Wenden
America Comes of Age
A. E. Campbell
Lenin's Path to Power
G. Katkov/H. Shukman
Weimar Germany
Sefton Delmer
Out of the Lion's Paw
Constantine FitzGibbon
Japan: The Years of Triumph
Louis Allen
Communism Takes China
C. P. FitzGerald
Black and White in South Africa
G. H. Le May
Woodrow Wilson
Edmund Ions
France 1918-34
J. P. T. Bury
France 1934-40
W. Knapp
Mussolini's Italy
Esmonde Robertson
The Little Dictators
A. Polonsky
Viva Zapata
L. Bethell
The World Depression
Malcolm Falkus
Stalin's Russia
A. Nove
The Brutal Reich
Donald Watt
The Spanish Civil War
Raymond Carr
Munich: Czech Tragedy
K. G. Robbins

Edmund Ions was born in North-umberland, and read Philosophy, Politics, and Economics at Merton College, Oxford. He was awarded a Harkness Commonwealth Fellowship to Harvard University, 1958-1960, and has since made further visits to Harvard, Columbia, and Stanford Universities as a visiting scholar. He now teaches at York University. His previous writings include *The Politics of John F. Kennedy* (1967), *James Bryce and American Democracy* (1968), and *Political and Social Thought in America, 1870-1970* (1970).

J.M.Roberts, General Editor of the Macdonald *Library of the 20th Century,* is Fellow and Tutor in Modern History at Merton College, Oxford. He was also General Editor of Purnell's *History of the 20th Century,* and is Joint-Editor of the *English Historical Review* and author of *Europe 1880-1945* in the Longman's History of Europe. He has been English Editor of the Larousse Encyclo-pedia of Modern History, has reviewed for *The Observer, New Statesman,* and *Spectator,* and given talks on the BBC.

Library of the 20th Century

Publisher: John Thompson
Editor: Richard Johnson
Executive Editor: Peter Prince
Designed by: Brian Mayers/ Germano Facetti
Research: Germano Facetti

Pictures selected from the following sources:

Culver Pictures 1 51 73 123
Imperial War Museum 57 76 78 106
Kladderadatsch 58 70
Library of Congress Cover 11 15 22 25 31 36 42 47 53 63 68 80 94 110 112 115 118 123
Mansell Collection 5 56 116 121
Museum of the City of New York 123
New York Times 56
Popperfoto 29 123
Punch 72 108
Radio Times Hulton 27 38 55 74 87 89 90 105
Simplicissimus 44 98
Smithsonian Institution 39
Suddeutscher Verlag 6 60 66
Ullstein 84
US Army 93
USIS 128
US War Department 64 81 83 122 123
Roger Viollet 89 96 102
Warshaw College of Business Americana 122

If we have unwittingly infringed copy-right in any picture or photograph reproduced in this publication, we tender our sincere apologies and will be glad of the opportunity, upon being satisfied as to the owner's title, to pay an appropriate fee as if we had been able to obtain prior permission.